Crime and Local Television News

Dramatic, Breaking, and Live
From the Scene

LEA'S COMMUNICATION SERIES
Jennings Bryant/Dolf Zillmann, General Editors

For a complete list of other titles in LEA's Communication Series, please contact Lawrence Erlbaum Associates, Publishers.

Crime and Local Television News

Dramatic, Breaking, and Live From the Scene

Jeremy H. Lipschultz
Michael L. Hilt
University of Nebraska at Omaha

LAWRENCE ERLBAUM ASSOCIATES, PUBLISHERS
2002   Mahwah, New Jersey   London

Lawrence Erlbaum Associates, Inc., Publishers
10 Industrial Avenue
Mahwah, NJ 07430

Cover design by Kathryn Houghtaling Lacey

Library of Congress Cataloging-in-Publication Data

Lipschultz, Jeremy Harris, 1958–
Crime and local television news : dramatic, breaking, and live from
   the scene / Jeremy H. Lipschultz, Michael L. Hilt.
         p. cm.—(LEA's communication series)
   Includes bibliographical references and indexes.
ISBN 0-8058-3620-9 (cloth : alk. paper)
ISBN 0-8058-3621-7 (pbk. : alk. paper)
1. Crime and the press—United States. 2. Television
   broadcasting of news—United States. I. Hilt, Michael L., 1959–
   II. Title III. Series.
PN4888.C8 L57 2002
070.4'49364—dc21

                                        2001057761
                                        CIP

Printed in the United States of America
10 9 8 7 6 5 4 3 2

Contents

About The Authors

Michael L. Hilt (PhD, University of Nebraska, 1994) and Jeremy H. Lipschultz (PhD, Southern Illinois University, 1990) are Professors of Communication at the University of Nebraska at Omaha. Hilt is Graduate Chair and the author of *Television News and the Elderly: Broadcast Managers' Attitudes Toward Older Adults* (New York: Garland, 1997). Lipschultz is the author of *Broadcast Indecency: F.C.C. Regulation and the First Amendment* (Boston: Focal Press, 1997), and *Free Expression in the Age of the Internet: Social and Legal Boundaries* (Boulder, CO: Westview, 2000).

The authors have written numerous scholarly articles in refereed publications such as *Journalism Quarterly, Journalism and Mass Communication Educator, Journal of Broadcasting and Electronic Media, Education Gerontology, Journal of Social Behavior and Personality, Journal of Radio Studies*, and *Communications and the Law*.

Before coming to Omaha in 1988, both Hilt and Lipschultz worked in broadcasting. Hilt worked in both radio and television news, including as a television news producer at KCTV in Kansas City, MO. Lipschultz worked in radio news, including as news director of WGBF–AM/WHKC–FM in Evansville, IN.

CONTRIBUTORS

Chris W. Allen (PhD, University of Missouri, 1996) is Assistant Professor of Communication at the University of Nebraska at Omaha.

Forrest Carr was News Director at KGUN–TV, Tucson, AZ, before moving to WFLA, Tampa, FL.

Lee Hood (PhD at the University of Colorado, 2001) is a former television news producer who now teaches broadcast news. Her research is on news audiences.

Mike McKnight is the Investigative Reporter at WOWT–TV, Omaha, NE.

Christine Mixan was a Graduate Teaching Assistant in Communication at the University of Nebraska at Omaha.

Jim Ogle is Vice President for News, WKYT–TV, Lexington, KY.

Angela Powers (PhD, Michigan State University, 1990) is Professor of Communication at Northern Illinois University.

Laura Shelton is a Reporter and Producer at KMTV–TV, Omaha, NE.

Foreword

Voyeuristic. Sensational. Pandering. For years, critics have used that kind of loaded language to describe the way television news covers crime. The criticism is driven in part by the disturbing images that often accompany crime stories on TV: body bags, blood-stained pavement, weeping relatives. But it's also based on the sheer quantity of the coverage, which tends to distort the frequency and significance of crime in local communities.

There is no question that crime stories dominate local television newscasts. Studies show that crime is the most frequently covered topic on local television and the most likely to be the lead story. That held true throughout the 1990s, despite the fact that the national rate of violent crime was declining. During that decade, for the first time, network newscasts reflected the same trend. The Center for Media and Public Affairs in Washington found that from 1990 to 1995, the number of crime stories on the three network evening news programs tripled—even without counting stories related to the O.J. Simpson case.

Television news also tends to connect crime and race in a way that does not reflect reality. Studies document that Blacks and other people of color are over represented as criminals on television and under represented as victims. Stories about crimes involving a Black perpetrator and a White victim get disproportionate coverage on television, compared to the actual occurrence of such crimes.

Social scientists say repeated exposure to this kind of coverage can leave viewers feeling numb or unreasonably paranoid about their chances of becoming a victim of crime, especially given the downward trend in crime statistics. "People should feel safer," Robert Lifton, professor of psychology at John Jay

College in New York, told the Los Angeles Times in 1999."But you really wouldn't know it from the news."

How did television news get so out of step with reality and what can be done about it? In *Crime and Local Television News*, Jeremy Lipschultz and Michael Hilt examine those questions and offer some proposals for reform. Their book distills decades of research about television news, and adds intriguing new findings based on surveys and content analysis, among them the importance of dramatic pictures of local origin in determining what gets on the air.

Television has always been driven by the need for pictures, and because crime stories are fairly visual stories, they are among the easiest for television journalists to produce. Never mind that the video is often predictable: flashing lights, yellow police tape, bystanders at the crime scene. At least there are pictures to be had. Crime stories also are prime candidates for live reporting, especially on the late evening newscasts when a crime story often is the closest thing to breaking news, something many stations now routinely promise their viewers.

The authors review other factors that impel local television to cover more crime than other types of stories. Local newsrooms tend to be staffed largely by young, highly mobile reporters and producers who lack the expertise required to cover important but complicated issues in a community they have lived in for only a year or two. Crime, alternatively, is a story even a new arrival can handle without much background knowledge, and one that can easily be told in the short amount of time usually allotted to any story in a television newscast.

Some critics link the emphasis on crime coverage to an almost desperate scramble for ratings by local stations beset by increased competition from cable channels. In the late 1980s, WSVN-TV in Miami became the poster child for building ratings success through tabloid news coverage. Lurid murders, shootings, stabbings and rapes often filled two-thirds of the news hole each night in a newscast *Newsweek* dubbed "Crime Time Live."As the violence quotient increased, the station's ratings did too. But by the mid-1990s, the formula had worn thin. Ratings dropped, and the station's emphasis shifted. A recent study found that WSVN-TV aired the least crime at 6 p.m. of any Miami station.

Research by NewsLab and others suggests that news managers are misguided if they believe they are responding to viewers' interests when they devote so much time to covering crime. In a national survey of self-described light television watchers conducted in 2000, almost a third said a major reason they did not watch more local TV news is that it covers too much crime—the biggest single reason given aside from issues of time and scheduling. Almost 60% said they would watch even less often if their local stations covered more crime.

Some stations have tried to reform their crime coverage, most notably KVUE-TV in Austin, TX, which in 1996, established a series of criteria that a crime story would have to meet before it could go on the air. Is the situation an immediate threat to public safety? Is it a threat to children? Do viewers need to take action? Does the crime have a significant impact on the community? And does the story suggest a crime prevention effort? This sensible screening process has yet to be widely adopted by other stations. In a more recent reform effort, Stephen Brill, publisher of the now-defunct media magazine *Brill's Content* proposed a code of conduct for reporters interviewing victims of crime. There was no rush to sign on.

Some journalists complain that efforts like these are tantamount to censorship. But advocates say they have not gone soft on crime. "We're not trying to deny the ugliness in the world; that's not what this is about," Kathy McFeaters, then executive producer at KVUE, told Columbia Journalism Review in 1996. "However, we have a responsibility not to give that ugliness more play than it deserves."

Even the most vocal critics would not urge television news to stop covering crime. After all, crime may be unpleasant but it is news. The real issue is *how* it's covered. As the authors of this volume make clear, television needs to do a better job providing viewers with context in stories about individual crimes, noting the rate of particular criminal acts and the risk factors associated with these crimes. Reporters should explore the causes and consequences of crime as vigorously as they do the actual commission of crimes. Their stories should include information about prevention efforts, as well. Beyond that, newsrooms should consider what stories they are missing—stories of greater importance to the communities they serve—when they concentrate so heavily on covering violent crime.

Indeed, it is long past time for television news to reexamine its coverage of crime. For years, television journalists have privately bemoaned their newsrooms' emphasis on sensational crime stories, but acted as if their hands were tied by inexorable market forces. Today, the tide may be turning. Newscasts have actually been losing viewers and are sticking to an outdated "if it bleeds, it leads" philosophy. And some stations like KGUN-TV in Tucson, AZ, that have changed their approach and de-emphasized crime have seen ratings gains.

Television news is a notoriously risk-averse business, one that favors imitation over innovation. Change comes slowly when it comes at all. By examining the reasons behind crime-intensive coverage on the local news, by assessing its effects and considering alternatives, this book gives news managers a strong incentive to choose a different path.

—*Deborah Potter*
NewsLab

Preface

The challenge of this book was to bring together the theory and practice of local television news. The industry experienced dynamic change since the 1970s, and mass communication theory is a useful framework for understanding the evolution.

As you read this book, several major themes are emphasized. Beyond the conceptualization of crime, the book considers local television news from a variety of perspectives. Initially, the literature and our anecdotal observation of local television news led us to focus on John McManus's idea of market-driven journalism. Although marketing remains important in the understanding of local television news today, we found other factors that were equally significant.

The need to be dramatic and visual, the emphasis on breaking news coverage, and the desire to be live from the scene may not be completely understood through the lens of marketing. Our survey data and the systematic examination of local newscasts from across the country suggested that local news, and specifically crime news, is also driven by news values and organization structure. News people appear to select stories they truly believe will be interesting to audience members, and they do this within a newsroom structure of decision makers. News consultants may help set a tone for that process, but it does not appear that they dictate an overall emphasis on crime.

Perhaps more telling is the day-to-day lack of interest in national news and public affairs coverage. It appears that except for unusual events—such as the September 2001 terrorism attack of the World Trade Center and the Pentagon—national and international news tends to be avoided. The need to be local and timely influences the decision to emphasize crime news. This is especially true in the late evening news broadcast when story choices are limited and government stories are hours old.

The introductory chapter explains the nature of local television news and the appeal of crime stories. In it, we highlight the majors themes of the book. Next, chapter 2 focuses on mass communication theory and its application to crime coverage. Chapter 3 looks at how local television stations often use crime news as a ratings builder. The structure of television news organizations is also considered. This chapter features original survey research data and content analyses of local television news broadcasts.

Chapter 4 examines legal issues in local television news. Crime coverage raises concerns about the First Amendment, access to crime scenes, and coverage of the courts. Ethical issues are discussed in chapter 5. Legal and ethical problems are addressed in the sixth chapter, which focuses on prisons and capital punishment. Chapter 7 is a case study of how one state dealt with three intensely covered executions during the 1990s.

Crime reporting and its relation with minorities and the elderly are highlighted in chapters 8 and 9. These are emerging issues in the research on local television news. As the average age of Americans goes up, local television news may be increasingly important in elevating fear of crime in society.

The book concludes with a chapter looking ahead. The future of local television news is clouded by social and technological change. Chapter 10 offers some proposals for reforming local television news and its coverage of crime.

The interdisciplinary study of local television news draws the reader to such areas as criminal justice, gerontology, and sociology. Much work needs to be done in the field of mass communication to fully integrate these concerns. Mass communication research in the future must be studied from a wide range of theoretical perspectives. At the same time, other fields have much to learn. In some cases, other disciplines have been more receptive to the integration of ideas.

The authors believe this book is useful to students studying to be broadcast journalists. If the industry is to change, its future employees will need to better understand social issues. Likewise, students of mass communication, media and society, public opinion, communication theory and research, and public relations and media management, would gain a better understanding of local television news by reading this book. Outside the field of journalism and mass communication, those interested in crime, race, aging, technology, law, and ethics also would find the case of local television news to be an instructive application.

ACKNOWLEDGMENTS

The authors wish to thank Communications Editor Linda Bathgate of Lawrence Erlbaum Associates for her careful review of the project. Reviewer Deborah Potter offered constructive comments on how to bring out the major themes of the work. The folks at Lawrence Erlbaum Associates have been extremely helpful and professional in guiding us through the project. In particular, Nadine Simms has done a wonderful job of guiding the manuscript to publication.

At the University of Nebraska at Omaha, our research on local television news was partially funded by the University Committee on Research, the Department of Communication, and the College of Arts and Sciences. The authors each benefitted from a generous professional leave from their teaching responsibilities at key points in the research process. Former Dean John Flocken and the College of Arts and Sciences, Communication Department Chair Deborah Smith-Howell, and the University of Nebraska Board of Regents, are thanked for their patience. Our colleagues in the Department of Communication have been very supportive of this research agenda.

Several teachers and scholars have directly influenced our thinking about local television news: Bill Miller, professor emeritus at the University of Illinois–Springfield, James Conyers and Jim Thorson at the University of Nebraska at Omaha, Vernon Stone, professor emeritus at the University of Missouri, James Fletcher at the University of Georgia, Rob McKenzie at East Stroudsburg University, and Frank Chorba at Washburn University.

Graduate student Christine Mixan assisted in the gathering of survey data and analysis of local television news content. The following people taped newscasts from around the country during the fall of 1999: Joel Anderson, Pamela Bennett, Larry Burkum, Paul Driscoll, Alan Eisenstein, Joel Fowler, Ed Freedman, Douglas Hindman, Lori Spiczka Holm, Lee Hood, Suzanne Huffman, Frank Imhoff, Mike Lipschultz, Paul Oehlke, Jim Ogle, Laura Shelton, and Deborah Smith-Howell.

The authors would like to thank their spouses and children. Jeremy's wife Sandy and children Jeff and Elizabeth were helpful with ideas about the importance of television in our society. Sandy's mom Faye and her enthusiasm for local television news offered a beneficial context. Mike's wife Debbie assisted in the proofreading. Debbie and the children, Adam and Eric, provided patience during the project. We love you all!

—*Jeremy H. Lipschultz*
—*Michael L. Hilt*
Omaha, Nebraska
December 2001

1

Introduction to Local Television News

"What do they get, the viewers who watch at 11 p.m.? They get local (news) 'with extreme prejudice,' to quote the old CIA term for authority to wipe out enemies. They get what Max Frankel of The New York Times *calls 'body bags at 11 o'clock, normally 30 minutes of hell and blather, ads and promos, local television's most profitable and most disheartening use of the air.'"*

—Robert MacNeil,
former PBS news anchor (1996, p. 7)

"Every day the particulars of television news—the news stories—are different, but the tone and feel of the newscast remains the same."

—Matthew R. Kerbel,
former producer and professor (2000, p. 130)

Viewers of local television newscasts across the country are regularly exposed to crime news stories. In this book, crime coverage is studied with an interest in how live reporting appeals to the desire to be dramatic and timely. For about 3 decades, crime stories within local TV newscasts have been nearly as common as weather and sports. Although marketing is a factor in the format of local TV news, it is also clear that news values and organizational structure drive a news culture that favors an emphasis on crime coverage.

Television in general, and local TV news in particular, are a part of everyday life. According to a recent Roper survey, 56% of Americans consider television to be their primary source for news (Roper Center, 1999b). Respondents who said they got most of their news about national and international issues from television identified three dominant sources: cable, local, and network TV news. Surprisingly, 39% said they turned to local TV news for national and in-

1

ternational stories, second only to cable news (Roper Center, 1999a). However, only 16% say local TV news is doing the best job of covering the news, behind cable and network TV (Roper Center, 1999c).

The criticism of local TV news has not turned viewers away from it. Local TV news is, of course, a local production that emphasizes what newsrooms perceive as interesting for themselves and their viewers. So-called "hard news" emphasizes "ongoing" events during the past day, and crime stories fit this model (Jamieson & Campbell, 2001, pp. 40–41). Violent crimes such as murders, robberies, and rapes

- Are definable events between individuals.
- Are dramatic, conflict-filled, and intense.
- Disrupt order and threaten the community.
- Are short, simple, and verifiable stories.
- Are visual and may be easily videotaped (p. 41).

Jamieson and Campbell (2001) reduce the crime story to five characteristics: (a) personalized through perpetrators and victims; (b) dramatic, conflict-filled, controversial, and violent; (c) actual and concrete; (d) novel or deviant; and (e) linked to issues of ongoing concern to media (p. 41).

The emphasis on breaking news, live shots, and sensational video tends to place a premium on crime reporting (Westin, 2000). For example, one 1993 to 94 study examined how KABC–TV, Los Angeles, covered crime and found that the station had an average of three crime stories per day (Gilliam, Jr., Iyengar, Simon, & Wright, 1996):

> The high level of violence was as expected: The overwhelming majority of news reports were episodic in nature and featured acts of violent crime.... Violent crime made up 30 percent of all crimes in Los Angeles County but was the focus of 78 percent of the news reports aired by KABC. (pp. 9–10)

Public opinion polls consistently find that a majority of Americans worry that crime is getting worse (Gallup Poll, 2000). Network television newscasts' coverage of murders increased by about 600%, although the national murder rate dropped by 20% between 1990 and 1998 (Westfeldt & Wicker, 1998), and the violent crime rate dropped by a record 10.4% in 1999 (Associated Press, 2000). No data exist for comparing local television news coverage of crime and local crime rates.

This book is about how and why local television news covers crime. Crime is considered "the most common and least studied staple of news" (Dennis & LaMay, 1992, p. xi). For more than 40 years, the Gallup Poll has found that Americans identify crime as either the first or second problem facing their local community. In the 2000 poll, 27% mentioned crime (including drugs, guns, and gangs) as "the worst problem" (Gallup Poll, 2000). If you turn on the local television newscast tonight, it is very likely that there will be at least one crime story. In fact, one study of the three dominant network affiliated stations in Chicago found that as much as 9 of the 14 minutes devoted to news "concerned the threat of violence to humans" (Entman, 1994b, p. 31). The coverage of crime is an everyday occurrence in local television newsrooms. Crimes such as murder, although not the most frequent form of crime, get the most attention because of their seriousness. Entman (1994b) offered the example of the murder of a child, allegedly by her mother, and a station's placing of the story in a "drug infested neighborhood" (p. 34). Local television news is seen as encoded to portray crime within a racial and economic context. By emphasizing crime in economically depressed neighborhoods, local newsrooms may reinforce stereotypes about minorities (Heider, 2000).

Although all of us have personal experiences as viewers, most of us do not pause to critically examine what we watch. This chapter provides an overview of local television news and the key concepts required for understanding it. We begin with the long-known view that

> Each of us lives and works on a small part of the earth's surface, moves in a small circle ... our opinions cover a bigger space.... They have, therefore, to be pieced together out of what others have reported and what we can imagine (Lippmann, 1922, 1965, p. 53).

THE NATURE OF LOCAL TV NEWS

Local television news is based on decisions made in newsrooms about what is newsworthy. "Although long overshadowed by the national media, local news has always played an important role in the way a city and region understands its problems, its opportunities, and its sense of local identity" (Kaniss, 1991, p. 2). News has typically been defined by criteria such as proximity, prominence, timeliness, impact, magnitude, conflict, and oddity (Ryan & Tankard, 1977, pp. 105–109). Not everyone agrees about the list. McManus (1994) included the following: timeliness, proximity, consequence, human interest, prominence, unusualness, conflict, visual quality, amusement, and topicality (pp. 119–120). Often, news is dominated by "known" as opposed to "unknown" people (Gans, 1979, p. 9). When officials and politicians are not the principal sources of stories, the unknown sources often are victims: "... Unknowns are victims of natural or social disorders, most often of crime, and on television, of tornadoes, floods, fires, plane accidents, and other natural or technological disasters" (Gans, p. 14). News selection involves "frames" for stories and use of a few newsworthy items from many choices (Tuchman, 1978). The metaphor of a "news net" being cast by editors offers one explanation:

> But a net has holes. Its haul is dependent upon the amount invested in intersecting fiber and the tensile strength of that fiber. The narrower the intersections between

The 2000 RTNDA convention in Minneapolis, MN, was the site for a blistering attack on television news. The meeting of news directors featured a keynote speech by Cable News Network correspondent Christiane Amanpour.

... All of us in this room share in this most ludicrous state of affairs. So much so that I recently carefully clipped a *New York Times* cutting and just about slept with it under my pillow.... WBBM–TV in Chicago is going back to basic journalism! A rare example of dog bites man actually being news!!!! And I have read of news directors in Florida and elsewhere around this country trying the same thing.

I don't dare ask how this radical experiment is doing in the ratings ... all my fingers and toes are tightly crossed.

At the end of the 20th century and the beginning of the 21st century, national television is the critical force. What we do and say and show really matters. It has an effect on our local communities, our states, our country, and on the state of the world.

You get the point... the powers that be ... the money men, have decided over the last several years to eviscerate us. It actually costs a bit of money to produce good journalism ... to travel, to investigate ... to put on compelling viewing, to give people a reason to watch us.

But God forbid they should spend money on quality ... no, let's just cheapskate our way into the most demeaning, irrelevant, super-hyped, sensationalism we can find. And then we wonder why people are tuning out in droves ... it's not just the new competition, it's the drivel we spew into their living rooms....

Network correspondent Christiane Amanpour speaking in 2000 to RTNDA.

... And there is so much good stuff being produced here in the United States ... but think how much more of a contribution we could make to this great society if we weren't so dependent on what those hocus-pocus groups tell us people are not interested in:

- Oh, Americans don't care about serious news.
- Oh, Americans don't care about this presidential election.
- Oh, Americans don't care about foreign news.
- Oh, Americans don't care about anything but contemplating their own navels.

H. L. Menken once said that no one would ever go broke underestimating the American people, but that's just flat out not true ... what Americans don't care much about is the piffle we put on TV these days, what they don't care about is boring, irrelevant, badly told stories, and what they really hate is the presumption that they are too stupid to know the difference. That's why they are voting with their off switch, which means that pandering to what we think people want is simply bad business. And we alienate our core constituency.

For example, why are we terrorizing the country at large leading with murder and mayhem when crime is actually on the decline?

Source: Radio-Television News Directors Association, News Release, http://www.rtnda.org/news/2000/asera.shtml

BOX 1.1.   CNN Correspondent Tells Local TV News Directors to Place News Quality above Profit Margins. (Photo courtesy Radio–Television News Directors Association, 2000)

the mesh—the more blanket-like the net—the more can be captured.... Today's news net is intended for big fish. (p. 21)

Crime news, particularly violent crime, is a staple for local television news. Since the 1970s, local television stations have invested in large newsrooms as "profit centers." Using "eyewitness" and "action news" formats, the news became a prime source of identity for local stations. These formats became successful in the television ratings by emphasizing crime news. The labels have been dropped, but the tone remains central to how local television stations cover the news today. The reliance on crime as "breaking news," "live," and "top stories" continues.

In this book we define crime broadly as behaviors that violate public laws designed to protect persons and property. Two competing models in criminal justice, due process and crime control, emphasize the innocence or guilt of the accused and the processing of defendants (Surette, 1998, pp. 15, 17). Local media coverage of crime and criminal justice are important because these images help lead to a social construction of reality: "People use knowledge gained from the media to construct an image of the world and behave based on the perceived reality of that image" (Surette, 1998, p. xiii). The use of police sources by local media to report crime stories may even lead to the social construction of a "crime wave" in a city, as Fishman (1980) observed in New York:

> Out of news work arose a phenomenon transcending the individual happenings which were its constituent parts. A crime wave is a "thing" in public consciousness which organizes people's perception of an aspect of their community.... The crime wave was also real in another sense. News organizes our perception of a world outside our firsthand experience. But in doing so, the media are not simply putting certain images in people's heads.... Even though one cannot be mugged by a crime wave, one can be frightened. (pp. 10–11)

Crime coverage, then, follows the structure and organization of police work that begins at the scene of a just-committed crime:

> Virtually all crime stories are about the commission of a crime (police report) and when a person is arrested (arrest report), charged with the crime (arraignment), brought to trial, convicted or acquitted, and, if convicted, sentenced. In other words, news is organized in exactly the same way as the criminal justice system "organizes" crime. And because it is organized that way and follows the same routines, the coverage tends to assume or take for granted the official organizational ideology. (Grossberg, Wartella, & Whitney, 1998, p. 331)

Local TV news emphasizes the earliest stage of crimes because "breaking news" from the scene of a crime is fresh, dramatic, and visual. A content analysis of local TV news, that will be reported in chapter 3, demonstrates how language such as "tonight's big story," "this just in," and "breaking news" functions to heighten drama. KXAS, Dallas–Ft. Worth, the NBC affiliate in Texas, for example, used narrative in this reporting from the scene:

> Sixteen houses make up this neighborhood. A close community where next weekend neighbors will gather for the annual fall festival. This evening, they gathered in concern, as word quickly spread that a teenager had been shot inside this home. Police carried out bags full of evidence. Neighbors were full of questions. The Monday afternoon quiet was pierced with screams. Apparently, one teen shot another teen with a 9-millimeter automatic pistol. Three hours after the screams and the gunshot rang out, police took away the crime scene tape, but not the questions. (October 11, 1999)

Live shots and on-set debriefings may stray from scripted copy, and this opens the door for reporter and anchor opinions. In Miami, FL, for example, a police drug sting led to a "gunfight" that resulted in two deaths. Fox affiliate WSVN questioned why police confiscated a videotape of the event by a cable TV channel:

Male anchor: I want to know about the idea of police officers going to a private citizen and confiscating his equipment without a warrant because that's what it sounds like the man is saying.

Reporter: The cameraman wasn't too happy about it. It doesn't happen very often. We're still trying to find out if this man will indeed get his tape back. Certainly he's captured some very interesting video.

Anchor: I imagine police aren't admitting to what this man describes, are they?

Reporter: Police haven't said anything to us regarding the tape....

Anchor: Hmmmm....

Reporter: ... but I did hear the cameraman talking to one of the police representatives on the scene ... so we'll see what happens with that tape ... but that cameraman did say he caught some very interesting things on it.... (October 12, 1999)

Video is a primary element in local TV news and supplements the use of charged language. In 1999, the following phrases were used: a dangerous chase; dramatic car crash, violent takeover robbery, terrifying ordeal, heartbreaking call, nightmare, tragedy; brutal ..., terror ..., desperate ..., terrorized ..., and disturbing.... In Kansas City, KS, ABC affiliate KMBC used a combination of live shots, video packages, and interviews in team coverage of the abduction of a 10-year-old girl and the police "manhunt" for the girl and a suspect. The stories included showing police searching a vacant house "with guns drawn" and a sound bite from the tearful mother of the victim pleading for return of her daughter. The next evening, the station again led with live team coverage from three reporters on the arrest of the suspect. The station showed video of the arrest scene:

> In the heavy brush alongside the Kaw River lies the metro's most wanted man. He was spotted on the river bank just after noon by this woman ... her husband and others went after him.... A two-day search finally reaches an end. (October 14, 1999)

The station broadcast interviews of eyewitnesses who saw the arrest. At the scene, they had video of a hospital helicopter arriving to transport the injured suspect.

The decision to cover a crime story is based on a set of organizational values. We speak of news values as being important in the construction of news: "Reporters use values to help them decide what information available for individual news stories should be used in the lead and what should be left out altogether" (Ryan & Tankard, 1977, p. 105). Herbert Gans (1979) formalized the idea of news values by grouping them into clusters:

The local television newsroom has been called a "news factory" because that metaphor describes mixed assembly-line work flowing through five steps: "story ideation, task assignment, gathering and structuring materials, assembling materials, and presenting the newscast" (Bantz, McCorkle, & Baade, 1980, p. 52). The routine nature of news production may lead to four negative aspects of organizational life:

1. The news factory lacks flexibility.
2. There is a lack of personal investment in the news product.
3. News work becomes evaluated in productivity terms.
4. Goal incongruence emerges between news workers' job expectations and job reality. (p. 59)

Although newsrooms may not be traditional assembly lines, they are subject to pressures to produce uniformity: "The trends in television news—the turnover of news workers, the influence of consultants, the producer supervision, the increased technical sophistication, increasing organizational size, and the emergence of the news as a profit center—have contributed to local television news' development of a highly constrained, routinized approach to news" (Bantz et al., pp. 64–65).

A research team of three people spent 14 weeks studying a local television station in the western United States. The story idea step involves assessing the raw information that comes into a newsroom, including the following:

• Press releases.
• Mail.
• Other media reports.
• Reporter enterprise ideas.
• Law enforcement and emergency radio traffic.
• News services.
• Telephone calls.

The assignment editor in a newsroom is the key person deciding what information should be presented at the news story meetings each morning. At the daily meetings, the assignment person, other news managers, and news staff meet to talk about story selection, coverage, and placement.

At the second step in the process, tasks are assigned to news staffers. Stations file story ideas as they arrive in the mail, over the telephone, by fax and via e-mail. For example, an organization may schedule a news conference days in advance and mail an announcement to the news department. Usually, one of the last duties of an assignment editor each day is to check the "future file" for leads on the next day's news. Early in the morning, potential stories are listed, discussed, and assigned to reporters and photographers.

The third step involves gathering and structuring news content. This involves reporters, photographers, producers, and editors. There are five tasks: (a) obtaining assignment desk information, (b) communicating with news sources, (c) going somewhere to gather background material, (d) shooting videotape, and (e) writing news copy.

The fourth step is assembling the raw material gathered into individual news stories. Raw video collected in the field must be edited to fit a news script written by a reporter. Reporters review the raw footage, if there is time, to determine what pictures fit the story and to select the sound bites from news makers. Once the script is finished, news managers may review it. Producers organize the stories from reporters and writers into a newscast. Stories may be edited further, ordered to create a flow, and fit to a particular format.

The last step is presenting the newscast. A production staff handles technical coordination of the elements. Although the news factory model generally is as valid now as it was a quarter-century ago, newsrooms today are more flexible in dealing with breaking news because of advances in live technology.

Source: Bantz, C. R., McCorkle, S., and Baade, R. C. (1980). The news factory. *Communication Research, 7,* 45–68.

BOX 1.2 The News Factory.

1. *Ethnocentrism.* Like the news of other countries, American news values its own nation above all, even though it sometimes disparages blatant patriotism.
2. *Altruistic democracy.* The news implies that politics should follow a course based on the public interest and public service.
3. *Responsible capitalism.* This is an optimistic faith that in the good society, business men and women will compete with each other in order to create increased prosperity for all, but that they will refrain from unreasonable profits and gross exploitation of workers or customers.
4. *Small-town pastoralism.* The news favors small towns over other types of settlements, reflecting historical rural American values.
5. *Individualism.* The preservation of the freedom of individuals should be guarded against the encroachments of nation and society.
6. *Moderatism.* This value discourages excess or extremism in favor of the middle ground.
7. *Social order.* The desirability of a certain type of social order is favored by the news.
8. *National leadership.* The need to maintain social order is rooted in the responsibility of our national leaders. (pp. 42–52)

The idea of social order over disorder is important in understanding why crime is a favored topic in local television newsrooms:

Social disorder news deals with activities which disturb the public peace and may involve violence or the threat of violence against life or physical property; it also includes the deterioration of valued institutions, such as the nuclear two-parent family. (Gans, 1979, p. 53)

Local violence, as portrayed on television through the news, suggests to the viewer that he or she may not be safe on the streets: "Crime news follows a similar cycle. An unusual crime story is particularly fresh, so much so that reporters are encouraged to find further examples, establishing a journalistic crime wave that may bear little relationship to the actual one" (Gans, 1979, p. 170). Today, crime coverage by local television newsrooms may be a function of market forces, rapid growth of competition from other stations, and the desire to produce content that draws viewers (McManus, 1994). Crime stories are easy to tell because they usually feature good and bad; innocent victims subjected to lawless behavior by criminals. Society, in a sense, is victimized by the inability of government to protect us from crime.

THE APPEAL OF CRIME NEWS

Research on the sociology of news work, as it relates to local television, has identified two key generalizations: (a) local news tends to rely on "routine" sources, including government officials and law enforcement personnel (Reese & Buckalew, 1995); and (b) competitive and corporate interests appear to "help *homogenize* the news rather than *diversify* it" (Ehrlich, 1995, p. 205). In the case of local TV news coverage of crime, it is predicted that selection of the same sources will lead to consonance in coverage. Given the dramatic nature of crime news, producers will tend to believe that these stories are good for station ratings because a large number of viewers should be interested.

Crime news, by one estimate, accounts for about 14% of local news coverage, and the lion's share of that coverage focuses on sensational events (Graber, 1993). Graber (1993) argued that the public, despite public complaints, has a hunger for exciting crime news: "The local television news, with its heavy crime component, has eclipsed national news, which carries more serious political stories and less crime, in the battle for high audience ratings" (p. 332). During the decade of the 1990s, crime stories appeared to take on increased importance for national viewers. A study of the top 10 news topics between 1990 and 1996 found that the networks (ABC, CBS, and NBC) covered crime more often (9,391) than any other story, even ahead of the economy (6,673), and health (6,047) issues (Hiebert & Gibbons, 2000, p. 248). In 1999, the shootings at Columbine High School in Littleton, CO, were followed "very closely" by 68% of Americans (Pew Research Center, 1999). The incident was the third most closely watched story of the decade, following coverage of the Rodney King verdict and riots in Los Angeles and the crash of TWA Flight 800 off the East Coast. In 1998, the top three closely watched stories were all crime stories: two school shootings, in Arkansas and Oregon, and a shooting at the U.S. Capitol.

Graber (1997) wrote that organizational factors are important in determining news making and reporting routines:

> Colleagues and settings strongly influence news people. Every news organization has its own internal power structure that develops from the interaction of owners, journalists, news sources, audiences, advertisers, and government authorities. In most news organizations today, the internal power structure is slightly left of middle America, yet predominantly supportive of the basic tenets of the current political and social system. (p. 96)

Kerbel (2000) maintained that newscast consistency is required in the local television news model: "If you know what to expect from a newscast, you'll become comfortable with it. Producers hope you'll even become a bit dependent on it" (p. 130). By delivering similar news stories, Kerbel suggested that newscast formats help explain what we see in the news.

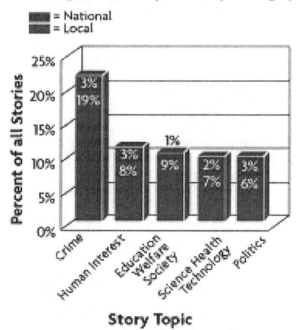

FIG. 1.1 Crime considered most important news topic in Project for Excellence in Journalism study. *Source:* The Project for Excellence in Journalism, 1999, used with permission.

THE SOCIOLOGY OF CRIME AND LOCAL TV NEWS

By dictionary definition, society defines crime as those serious behaviors that violate public laws. In the United States, crime is measured by the Federal Bureau of Investigation (FBI) Uniform Crime Reports (UCR). The government defines violent crime as murder or manslaughter, rape, robbery, assault, burglary, large theft, and, in some cases, arson (Brownstein, 2000). The concept of violent crime is fuzzy because, like crime itself, violence can be recognized without an explicit definition: "This is true in part because violence is not just one thing but rather many things, making it easier to give examples of violence than to say exactly what it is" (Brownstein, 2000, p. 6).

The examples of crime and violence portrayed by local TV newscasts play a role in defining the nature of criminal activity in society. The dramatic nature of crime coverage is the source of much criticism:

> Crime, violence, and tragedy have become staples of local newscasts, leading to the catchphrase, "If it bleeds, it leads".... During the newscast, the anchors deliver the horrifying details, look solemn for a moment, and then swing into "happy talk" with one another. They address the camera earnestly in an attempt to establish contact with the home viewer. It is a curious mix of camaraderie and concern, all delivered somewhat breathlessly and with almost no context provided for the viewer. (Hiebert & Gibbons, 2000, p. 247)

The mass media seem to be a major source of information people use to develop views about social issues such as crime. "In this way, the media have played an indirect but significant long-term role in shaping people's thoughts and actions" (DeFleur & Dennis, 1996, p. 595). Where media messages are consonant, it is possible that the content will have the effect of influencing people (Noelle-Neumann, 1995).

It has been argued that the mass media are willing participants in creating social myths:

> The social construction of myths of crime and criminal justice seems to follow a series of recurrent patterns. These patterns allow for an unprecedented amount of social attention to be focused upon a few isolated criminal events or issues. This attention is promoted by intense, but often brief, mass media coverage of a select problem (Kappeler, Blumberg, & Potter, 1993, pp. 4–5).

This idea is related to the view that mass media portrayals construct social reality for individuals and groups. Surette (1992) argued that our collective view of prisons and prisoners is shaped by entertainment portrayals, and news coverage appeals to "voyeuristic instincts" (pp. 41, 74). Ultimately, such a portrait supports law-and-order policies and becomes "the accepted version of social reality" (p. 76).

It was not always the case that local television news crime coverage overwhelmed reporting of issues. A combination of business practices, technological changes, and news formatting opened the door to what we see on local television news today.

RISE IN LOCAL TV NEWS
POPULARITY AND SIGNIFICANCE

During the 1950s and 1960s, few local television news operations were profitable. Then, in 1970, the ABC network affiliate in Sioux City, IA, showed that by investing in the local newsroom, viewer loyalty could increase ratings and profits (Westin, 2000). During the 1970s, the "Eyewitness News" format emphasized reporting from the scene of events and use of film and video (Fang, 1985, p. 317). The format was developed by Al Primo at WABC-TV, New York, as a way to boost ratings by more than 10%. The success in New York led to dozens of copies around the country (Dominick, Wurtzel, & Lometti, 1975). The format highlighted reporters covering events and then doing live reports featuring interaction with anchors. At times, this led to emphasis on crime coverage, according to one study of three network flagship stations in New York in 1973: "... the Eyewitness staff went out of its way to find and report violent stories that the other two stations chose not to report" (Dominick, Wurtzel, & Lometti, 1975, p. 216). The researchers found that the ABC station was much more likely than the CBS or NBC stations to emphasize crime, and this was criticized: "Emphasizing violent, human interest and comic material, in an apparent effort to gain larger ratings may not be in the public interest" (Dominick, Wurtzel, & Lometti, 1975, p. 218).

The success of Eyewitness News spawned other similar variations on the packaging of local TV newscasts. The "Action News" format of shorter and tighter stories took advantage of the "Electronic News Gathering" (ENG) live technology and videotape (Head, Sterling, Schofield, Spann, & McGregor, 1998, p. 263). Local television newsrooms began to purchase live trucks and even helicopters for covering breaking spot news from the scene. During the 1980s and 1990s, a "technological wave" continued—smaller and lighter cameras, computerized newsrooms, digital editing and effects, portable microwave live links, and stylized graphics (Eastman & Ferguson, 1997, p. 206). At the same time, competitive pressures and news consulting encouraged coverage of breaking crime news as part of a trend begun in the early 1970s (Barrett, 1975). The model turned network affiliated local stations into "cash calves" bought and sold for more than $500 million (Dominick, Sherman, & Messere, 2000, p. 100). In a profit-driven environment, the importance of news consultants is that they may encourage the use of more local stories, live remotes, and disaster coverage; however, this may not always lead to more crime coverage (Harmon, 1999).

These changes suggest the need for a fresh study of local television news that is informed by both industry practices and academic investigation. This book makes the case for the importance of crime coverage in understanding the nature of local television news. Social science and critical and cultural media theories help explain why local television news finds crime stories so compelling and irresistible.

CHAPTER SUMMARY

Crime news is an important component of local television newscasts. The organizational need to be dramatic helps explain why crime is frequently featured. At the same time, the public consistently expresses concern about crime while continuing to use local TV news as a key source for information. Given the importance of news values and organizational structure, it is likely that the model of local television news forged during the 1970s will continue. Live technology allows stations to efficiently report from the scene of breaking local news events.

DISCUSSION QUESTIONS

1.   How would you define local television news? Why is it important?
2.   How has local television news evolved to emphasize crime news?
3.   Why is crime news an important staple in lead stories on local television news?
4.   Why are crime and violence difficult to define?
5.   In your opinion, what role should crime news play within the daily decision-making process in a local television newsroom?

2

Theory and Research
on Crime News

"The media and crime and justice must all be approached as parts of larger phenomena that have numerous interconnections and paths of influence among them."

—Ray Surette, media scholar (1998, p. 2).

To understand the importance of crime to local television news, it is essential to have a framework. In chapter 1, we introduced the nature of local television news and its rise in popularity and significance during the past 30 years. As local stations placed greater emphasis on news gathering, the broadcasts evolved from basic headline summaries to highly produced shows. The industry came to rely on consultant research to help mold and shape local newscasts. At the same time, university researchers began to study the news process. This chapter focuses on mass media research as it relates to crime news on local television. Theories and concepts about news will help explain why crime stories play such a prominent role in local newscasts. Throughout this book, the theories discussed here will be referenced as a way to better understand local TV news coverage of crime from a social perspective.

CRIME NEWS IN THE AGE OF TELEVISION

The portrayal of crime news on local television is a "part of the spectacle of everyday life" (Kidd-Hewitt, 1995, p. 1). It is believed that the amount of crime news on local television exceeds the amount found in newspapers and on national television newscasts (Surette, 1998). Graber (1980) estimated that crime news accounted for nearly 20% of the total news coverage at two Chicago television stations (the CBS- and NBC-owned stations) in 1976. There has been no systematic attempt to measure trends during the past 2 decades, or to collect generalizable data for local television news markets. Still, Graber's research is useful in identifying topics of crime news coverage—police and security, judiciary, corruption and terrorism, and individual crime; and the reporting of various types of crime—street crimes, terrorism, corruption, drug offenses, and business crimes (Graber, 1980, pp. 24, 36):

> Crime news receives ample coverage and display compared to other types of news. By certain social significance criteria, it is excessive. However, if current notions about audience preferences are accurate—and readership and viewer data seem to support them—then ample coverage of crime news can be justified as satisfying a strong consumer demand. (pp. 40, 42)

In general, it can be said that crime is central to local television news gathering, and the result is that audience members see a lot of crime news coverage (Chermak, 1994). What viewers see in the newscasts may be perceived as real. The literature refers to this as social construction of reality.

SOCIAL CONSTRUCTION OF REALITY

Social construction of reality maintains the philosophical view that "all symbolic universes and all legitimations are human products; their existence has its base in the lives of concrete individuals, and has no empirical status apart from these lives" (Berger & Luckmann, 1966, p. 128). The theory, in more recent times, has been linked to research on television. At one level, local television news producers construct a reality through the decisions made about the coverage of events and their placement within a newscast. At another level, viewers construct their own realities by interpreting news through a set of personal experiences. Lang and Lang (1984, p. 26) generalized the following:

1. Television emphasizes close-up views creating a sense of familiarity with distant people and places.
2. Live event coverage gives viewers a sense of participation in public affairs.
3. Television pictures seem authentic to viewers.
4. Television coverage may provide a more complete picture of the event than any other media.

In general, "the act of making news is the act of constructing reality itself rather than a picture of reality" (Tuchman, 1978, p. 12). The construction of reality in local television news begins with the newsroom decision to cover a story. It continues when the reporter and photographer arrive at the scene of a story, and they gather raw material. Social construction of news also involves editing and producing a story for broadcast. The social construction of crime news is symbolic, and it is a form of news gathering useful in the production of social reality:

> Media images or characterizations of crime and crime control in the United States are constituted within the core of the social, political, and psychological makeup of American society. Mass news representations in the "information age" have become the most significant communication by which the average person comes to know the world outside his or her immediate experience. (Barak, 1994, p. 3)

Crime stories, as represented in local television newscasts, are useful in the culture as a way to define societal norms of behavior: "... as a result it is often difficult, if not impossible, to separate the perception of crime and the reaction to crime" (Barak, 1994, p. 32). Local television news constructions essentially distribute knowledge to a local community in ways that influence decision making, create a "dominant" social product, and lead to a social construction of reality that "steers public policy" (Surette, 1998, p. 11). Social construction of reality is one theoretical perspective among many that are useful in helping us understand the nature of local television news.

PSYCHOLOGICAL AND SOCIAL IMPACT OF CRIME AND VIOLENCE

Research in the fields of psychology, sociology, and communication is particularly helpful in making generalizations about how local television news viewers might use media content, and what benefits they might receive:

> The psychologists asked how communication affected individuals or small groups. The sociologists asked how communication affected organizations and societies. The result was that communication became ... referred to as a "variable field," one in which the level of analysis varies. (Lang, 1994, p. vii)

As applied to local television news, this means that we need to draw from a variety of fields to understand the significant role local newscasts play in defining social reality in communities. For example, psychologists study individual differences in the ways that viewers look at the television screen, and this may help explain why viewers retain different information (Anderson & Burns, 1991). It is necessary to examine the importance of active audience members in defining the realities they take from watching the local newscast.

Uses and Gratifications

During the past 30 years, one of the central issues of media studies has been what people do with news content. As such, so-called uses and gratifications research works from basic assumptions:

1. Television news viewers have psychological and social needs.
2. Television news viewers expect to have certain experiences when they view the local newscasts.

Kyle Bell was convicted in the summer of 1999 of molesting and killing an 11-year-old Fargo, ND, girl in 1993. Her body was never found, but Bell told police he dumped her body in a river. Bell was sentenced to life in prison. While being transferred to an Oregon prison, he escaped on October 13, 1999, in New Mexico. Thus began the transformation of an isolated local crime story to a regional and then national event.

KXJB–TV, the CBS affiliate in Fargo, led its late evening newscast with the Bell escape. He escaped at a truck stop while being moved by a private company that "ships prisoners across the country." The station took a live feed from the CBS affiliate, KRQE, in Albuquerque, NM.

That same night, KOAT–TV, in Santa Fe, NM, led with the "manhunt" for Bell. The escapee, described as a "dangerous murderer," was being transported from North Dakota when he used a key to get loose in Santa Rosa, NM. The station showed Christmas Eve home video of the victim from before her death.

The Fox Television Network program *America's Most Wanted* featured the Bell escape in a January 8, 2000, segment. Bell escaped through a ventilation hatch while guards were taking an extended break, the program reported. He had reportedly last been seen 2 days after the escape in a Wisconsin bar.

After *America's Most Wanted* aired the story and Kyle Bell's photo, a husband and wife in a Dallas, TX, apartment complex called the hotline after recognizing their neighbor. FBI agents arrested Bell early the next day. He had been living in the apartment for 2 months with a woman and her five children. Although Bell had shaved his head and mustache, he had four identifying tattoos—the Grim Reaper, a Panther, a Heart, and a Winged Horse.

Bell was the 596th person captured after being featured on *America's Most Wanted*. The reality program often uses local crime stories in which suspects or convicts are on the loose. These are social constructions of reality that rarely are reported in traditional network news.

Sources: *America's Most Wanted*, http://www.amw.com (January 8, 2000); KOAT–TV, Santa Fe, NM (October 13, 1999); KXJB–TV, Fargo, ND (October 13, 1999); Chris Graves, "Escaped Killer Bell Arrested," *Minneapolis Star Tribune* (January 10, 2000), p. 1A.

Convicted killer Kyle Bell.

BOX 2.1   Local TV News Crime Coverage Goes National.
(Photo of Kyle Bell courtesy of North Dakota law enforcement officers.)

3. Television news viewers make decisions about viewing based on their expectations.
4. Television news viewers make future viewing decisions based on how well their needs were gratified, and this may lead to "unintended" consequences (Palmgreen, Wenner, & Rosengren, 1985, p. 14).

The uses and gratifications model proposes that audience members are active in making decisions about what to watch, and how to watch it. McQuail (1985) contended that uses and gratifications research meets the needs of media scholars, practitioners, and audience members wishing to understand the lure of mass media:

> Viewed this way, the business of trying to find out what people are getting from their media experience and what their motives are seems a straightforward matter, requiring no more theoretical justification, attack, or defense than does the counting of audience members and the description of audience composition. (p. 150)

However, there has been a lot of debate about the nature of this sort of research. Although the idea that audience members play an active role in the local television news viewing experience seems obvious, uses and gratifications research is a descriptive model that falls short of helping us to understand the varied motivations of viewers. Although audience members may actively make choices about which channel, if any, they watch for local news, once there they must rely on the choices of news producers about what is important.

Agenda Setting

Agenda setting, the idea that mass media tell people what to think about rather than what to think, is a research tradition developed by Maxwell McCombs and Donald Shaw in 1972. In that study, "law and order" was the second most important issue behind "foreign policy" (Severin & Tankard, 2001, p. 236). Since then, hundreds of published articles have attempted to measure media and public issue agendas, and the relation between the two (Ghanem, 1997). The framing of agendas by local television may lead stations to avoid political stories as boring, and searching for crime news stories that are usually accompanied by dramatic video. The play of exciting video may feed into viewers' interpretations, or what the research calls cognitive schema: "They extract only those limited amounts of information from news stories that they consider important for incorporation into their schemata" (Ghanem, 1997, p. 8). The schema, in other words, is a long-term way of thinking about the world. Agenda setting, then, is related to the decisions that news people make within their organizations (Gandy, 1982). In a broad sense, media portrayals cultivate "the adoption of a particular point of view that is more in line with media presentation than with reality" (Ghanem, 1997, p. 9). For example, portrayal of African

American crime suspects may prime viewers by reinforcing racial stereotypes. In this way viewers may overestimate the share of violent crime committed by non-Whites.

Agenda setting is limited as a perspective because it fails to account for potentially strong influences on audience members. In local television news, the agenda is likely to be affected by a complex interaction between events, news judgments, and available time and resources. It is known that breaking crime news stories have the possibility of becoming lead story material, but that does not explain the phenomenon. Likewise, cognitive information processing theories such as agenda setting tend to emphasize the limited amount of information retained by viewers. In this way, agenda setting may oversimplify and downplay the viewers' involvement. In the long term, viewers may not recall specific stories, but they may be "learning" something about their communities through watching local newscasts. For example, regular viewing of crime stories may cultivate fear or anxiety.

Cultivation Research

The work of George Gerbner and his associates treats mass media content as having a direct impact on viewers:

> In its simplest form, cultivation analysis tries to ascertain if those who spend more time watching television are more likely to perceive the real world in ways that reflect the most common and repetitive messages and lessons of the television world, compared with people who watch less television but are otherwise comparable in important demographic characteristics. (Morgan & Signorielli, 1990, p. 16)

> That means that television's independent contribution to such patterns is most likely to be in the direction of homogeneity within otherwise different and diverse social groups, eroding traditional social and other distinctions.... It means that large and otherwise comparable groups of regular television viewers from different walks of life share a stable commonality of meanings compared to the lighter viewers in the same groups, and the commonality reflects their exposure to the television mainstream, eroding other traditional group differences. (Gerbner, 1990, pp. 260–261)

In cultivation research, we are interested in how the amount of television viewing impacts a person's "conception" of social reality: "The basic hypothesis is that heavy viewers will be more likely to perceive the real world in ways that reflect the most stable and recurrent patterns of portrayals in the television world" (Morgan & Signorielli, 1990, pp. 9–10). "Heavy" viewers of dramatic television content are hypothesized in cultivation research to be linked with their exaggerated estimates of victimization (Ogles & Sparks, 1989). In the case of local television news viewing, cultivation theory would suggest that "heavy" viewers of local news would draw conclusions about life in their communities based on what they see in the newscast. For example, if crime is a dominant feature of the newscast, then "heavy" viewers ought to perceive their towns or cities as violent, dangerous, or even "scary" places to live. "Crime on television is the work of strangers and madmen who, at any moment, select one of us at random to be their victim" (Howitt, 1998, p. 45). If the cultivation hypothesis is correct, then these viewers should use the content they see as a gauge of how safe they feel in and out of their homes. Ultimately, such views should influence viewer behavior. If viewers are afraid because of what they see on local television news, then they should be more likely to lock their doors, invest in security systems, and light their property at night. At the same time, they should be less likely to take a neighborhood walk, open their doors to strangers, and leave their homes for extended periods of time. However, local television news viewing is one source among many factors that might influence these behaviors. Actual neighborhood crime, including personal experience as a victim of crime, should also be influential.

CULTURAL STUDIES AND MEANING MAKING

From a broader perspective, there are two communication models: transmission and cultural. The transmission model is the traditional linear view of communication that focuses on how media messages are sent to the audience. In contrast, the cultural model emphasizes shared meanings and spaces: "Without this common reality, communication would be impossible, and in fact, the vast majority of our communication merely serves to ritualistically reproduce that system of shared meanings within which we live" (Grossberg, Wartella, & Whitney, 1998, p. 20). In this view, we take for granted the role that culture plays in helping us make sense of what we see in mass media. In the case of local television news, a community must be able to share the meanings of the stories that newscasters tell. When they report crime stories, viewers may be able to infer subtle meanings that place events within the context of their lives. Race, income, education, and geographic differences will make a difference in the ways that crime stories are interpreted. Somewhat related is the importance that "scandal" has in television news: "Within the complexities, uncertainties and threats of postmodernity, the scandal functions simultaneously as a moral anchor in a sea of conventionality, and as a vigorous challenge to mainstream social values conditioned by the substantial forces of ideological and cultural hegemony" (Lull & Hinerman, 1997, p. 2). Crime news focuses on the risky, dangerous nature of the world, whereas scandal may refocus our attention away from our own fears and toward the dangers faced by public people. There are times when crime and scandal intersect. For example, Los Angeles television newsrooms dealt with such a story during coverage of the O. J. Simpson case. When a well-known public figure becomes embroiled in a murder case, the events can be catapulted onto the national media stage.

For more than a century, news coverage in America has been evolving from a public affairs orientation to a more popularized, event-driven model: "The content became less focused on politics and more on crime, human interest, and sensational content" (Grossberg et al., 1998, p. 324). In the case of local television news, timeliness has become a preeminent news value:

> In part, the technologies help account for why news becomes event-centered rather than discursive: A reporter on the scene of an event "covers" that event and transmits a report to a newsroom, rather than digesting it and other events for later writing. And media compete with each other to bring the latest news to audiences first. (Grossberg et al., p. 325)

Recall in chapter 1 that we listed the factors that determine the newsworthiness of a potential story. Here it is important to apply these criteria to the selection of crime news in a local television newscast. Crime news can be seen as a form of conflict; two or more people are engaged in an action in which at least one party suffers. Violent crime is highlighted in the news because harm has been done not only to individuals but also to society. The aftermath of a crime produces a scene particularly suited for television news—bright lights, emotionally-charged sound-bites from eyewitnesses or police, a mystery of what happened, a lot of activity by detectives, and other out-of-the ordinary events captured on videotape. "Unexpected" spot news stories often have a short life span (McQuail, 2000, p. 282, citing Tuchman, 1978), and "drama and action" are important in determining news values and the "framing" of news (McQuail, 2000, p. 342).

Crime news is a question of judgment by a writer or producer of a local television newscast. The assessment of the impact of a potential story is in part a judgment on how many people are affected, as well as the types of people involved. Well-known individuals serve as a magnet for all types of news coverage. The prominence of people in the news—politicians, entertainers, athletes, community leaders—becomes relevant because they are easily-identifiable to viewers as the people at the top of the social structure. Crime news is often an unexpected event that is seen by news producers as strange or unusual. It is important to distinguish an isolated, bizarre incident that captures momentary attention from larger crime themes such as a series of bank robberies, arson fires, child abductions, and school shootings. In these examples, media track what appear to the casual observer to be a trend in society, whether or not in fact it turns out to be the case. In some cases, local television newscasts use "We" as a way of constructing "… their authority to tell moralizing stories" (Baym, 2000, p. 92). Anchors serve as both authoritative professionals and as the voice of the local community: "By speaking with the voices of both institutional authority and communal believability, journalists construct their right to mediate; affirming their position as agents of the people, moral watchdogs entrusted with the power to police the borders of proper behavior" (Baym, 2000, p. 109).

Two other factors that are often linked when judging the newsworthiness of a potential story are the timeliness of the story, and its proximity to the local viewing audience. "Breaking news" is valued by news producers because it is a form of crime news that

1. Allows the viewer to be taken to the scene of an event as it is happening.
2. Excites some viewers with anticipation about the unexpected.
3. Provides fresh content from previous newscasts particularly suited for news promotion leading into the newscast.
4. Uses video that is a departure from routine shot selection and editing because it must be done quickly.
5. Creates "live-from-the-scene" reports—a "real" setting as a backdrop for the news, different from the station's news set.

By definition, local television news tends to draw from the immediate viewing area for its content. Local content is assumed interesting to viewers, and it is also accessible to newsrooms under deadline pressure. Station resources such as availability of live trucks, videographers, reporters, and engineers affect the decision to cover a breaking event.

Gans's (1979) national news values are broader than newsworthiness criteria: "ethnocentrism, altruistic democracy, responsible capitalism, small-town pastoralism, individualism, moderatism, social order, and national leadership" (p. 42). Ethnocentrism relates to values that emphasize American culture; altruistic democracy emphasizes public interest and service; responsible capitalism trusts the business community; small-town pastoralism yearns for the simplicity of rural life; the preservation of individualism helps promote freedom; moderatism discourages extremism; social order is displayed through routine coverage of day-to-day politics, as well as the threats to social order; and the need for national leadership is portrayed as a means to maintain social order.

Crime news can be seen as threats to the social order and examples of social disorder. "Social disorder news deals with activities which disturb the public peace and may involve violence or the threat of violence against life or physical property" (Gans, 1979, p. 53). For example, local news coverage of the rise in street gang activities such as drive-by shootings can be seen as threats to the existing social order in a community. At the same time, long-term coverage may link particular or even isolated events to trend themes that offer viewers a social barometer of conditions in their community:

> Social disorder is generally defined as disorder in the public areas of the society. A protest march in which three people die would be headline national news, whereas a family murder that claimed three victims would be a local story. Disorders in affluent areas or elite institutions are more likely to be reported then their occurrence elsewhere. (Gans, 1979, p. 58)

For local television news, a murder of a wealthy suburban family is newsworthy and would raise larger community issues about safety. As this hypothetical story unfolds, competing stations rush crews to the scene to establish live video

Local Television Reporter Reflects on Crime Coverage, by Laura Shelton

It doesn't take long in the news business before your sense of hearing changes. You begin to listen to more and more things at once. Somehow you grow accustomed to following all three of your competitors' 6 o'clock lead stories. You're able to hear the distinctive tones of disaster no matter how far you are from the scanner. In a heartbeat you're scribbling an address, grabbing a photographer, and running out the door. You're dashing headlong toward the lead story, racing the clock and the competition to bring your coverage to the audience. It's an adrenaline pumping frenzy. It's why many of us are in this business. And it's what can get you into trouble.

Reporters aren't too popular with the public. Faith in the news industry is on the decline. You get a lot of it when you're covering crime stories—the hostile stares, sometimes the obscene shouts for you to leave them the **** alone. How did our eager rush out of the newsroom translate into our vicious "vulture" status on the street? It didn't come from the stories we did about the summer camp for kids with cancer or the blind man who sells handmade brooms for a living. They're not mad about our coverage of the latest road construction that could slow them down on their morning commute. It all comes from the crime coverage.

To those in the news business, covering crime seems vital. Many of us equate crime with news. But we rarely stop to ask ourselves if this is really something people want to know about. Will hearing about the latest bank holdup really hold the audience's attention, and will it matter to them? It has the visual elements to make news with the line of police tape and the fuzzy picture from surveillance video, but does it matter to the audience?

Recent viewer surveys have shown that people don't like hearing about random acts of violence. The more they see them, the more violent they assume the world is, and the less they feel they can do about it. What we in the news business may see as solid journalism, the public might just see as more evidence that they are truly living in a violent society and are helpless to change it.

No matter what story I'm covering, I try to retain my integrity and let the stories retain theirs as well. In order to do that, there are some specific things I keep in mind while dashing out the door of the newsroom: First, and most important, is to stop, take a breath, and remember the story. It seems pretty basic but unless you keep yourself focused, you can get caught up in the mad dash and lose sight of everything else. Walking onto the scene of a shooting you can't just look for facts. Emotions are involved and you have to carefully balance those emotions to produce a good story.

The second point to keep in mind is the impact of the story. You have to be able to tell a story that you could be comfortable with if you were sitting there watching it with those involved. Don't let others dictate your story, but make sure the finished product is something you stand behind and something worthy of defending.

These aren't things I get reminded about very often. News directors simply don't have much time to play coach. Instead, these are things you may have learned in school, in an ethics seminar, or from people with more experience in the business. They will help you be better at your job whether you're covering crime or fluff. The only one in charge of playing watchdog is you. The public might take over occasionally, and when they do, if you're covering your stories with a conscience, remembering who they impact and keeping them balanced, you'll have an easier job defending your own work.

Viewers rely upon the images of crime news coverage as reality, but news people have limited access to a crime scene. "Television's reputation as a visual medium for news is based disproportionately on some extraordinary pictures …, on routine disaster coverage, on 'shooting bloody' in war; but in the bulk of the stories, most actual pictures are decorative and illustrative …" (Gitlin, 1980, p. 265). In our hypothetical crime scene, local television news crews will be placed at a distance from where the crime was committed, and separated from victims and police by yellow crime scene tape. The pictures will be limited to any available movement. Television news pictures are framed by the limits of the camera and existing technology, as well as by the numbers of and position of photographers at the scene. In recent years, the limits of technology have expanded. Some local television stations have attached a camera to the top of live trucks for an above-the-scene shot. Other stations use cameras mounted on TV towers or tall buildings. Video can also be gathered through the use of hidden cameras, as well as shots from airplanes and helicopters. The images viewers see eventually are edited into a formula for storytelling—wide shot to show the relationship of the story subject to its surroundings, the medium shot to take a closer look, and the close-up shots to depict emotion in a way that creates an illusion of intimacy. There is a moral component to local television news. On the one hand, there are stories about institutional scandals or celebrities. On the other hand, coverage of scandals that involve "moral violations by 'ordinary people'" may be seen as stereotypical "psychodrama":

These scandals are not about celebrities, but the stories they entail frequently make stars out of ordinary people. While the star scandal makes the indiscretions of well-known persons public, the psychodrama scandal turns ordinary persons who do extraordinary things into public figures. Two ingredients are crucial. First, the psychodrama scandal story must be compelling in a particular way, and, second, the characters ("stars") should reflect stereotypes fitting to the story. (Lull & Hinerman, 1997, p. 22)

BOX 2.2   Local Television Reporter Reflects on Crime Coverage, by Laura Shelton, reporter and producer, KPTM–TV, Omaha, NE (1999), and KMTV–TV, Omaha, NE (2000–2001).

links with their newsrooms. It would be necessary to obtain and air video from the scene. In television, previous research on coverage of social disorder has shown that, "Audiences with less direct experience of the situations at issue were more vulnerable to the framings of the mass media" (Gitlin, 1980, p. 245).

Local television news today is impacted by economic factors of the marketplace, as well as by journalistic norms. McManus (1994) contended that there are two models for explaining news production decision making:

1. The market approach requires bias in stories affecting the interests of the media firms' advertisers, parent corporation, and investors. In contrast, journalism requires the news be told with as little bias as humans can manage.

2. The journalistic theory contains no element of cost or payment, while the economic theory has the word "cost" or "pay" ... and cost is implied in the word "harm".... The journalistic model is unconcerned about what it costs to discover what's happening in a community (p. 86).

McManus (1994) theorized that news production may be understood by merging market theory and journalistic theory. When this is done, we can predict the probability that an event or issue will become news. McManus predicted that if an event or issue would have an adverse effect on advertisers, investors, or the corporation itself, then it should be less likely to be covered as news. Likewise, the higher the cost of covering and reporting an event or issue, the less likely producers should be to consider it newsworthy. Production decisions are based, in part, on assembly costs (Lacy & Bernstein, 1992). However, the higher the appeal of the story to the audience, the more likely it is to be attractive to advertisers, and thus considered newsworthy. McManus suggested that, "... the money spent investigating a sex scandal involving an important public official might justify its cost by attracting audience away from competitors" (p. 87). McManus's "market-driven journalism" model helps explain why local television news is increasingly attracted to scandal, sensationalism, and society at its worst. Although McManus does not directly address crime as a concept, his explanation of news production is a useful model for predicting an emphasis of crime coverage on local television news.

Chermak (1994) looked extensively at crime news coverage by newspapers. The daily reporting of crime news helps to raise public concern about crime in a community. Crime has been found to be one of the most frequent types of news stories, along with sports, general interest, and business reporting. Chermak (1994, pp. 104–109) listed five explanations for the "prevalence" of crime news:

1. It "provides the public with protection and knowledge."
2. It serves as a "deterrent," based on the assumption that "potential criminals pay attention to the news."
3. It serves as entertainment, capitalizing "on the public's fascination with gore and pathos."
4. It reflects the nature of criminal justice in that television would have a "steady supply of newsworthy crime stories."
5. It fills a relatively large news hole by utilizing available public sources.

For local news organizations, there are three stages in the criminal justice process that appear to make up nearly half of all crime news stories: the discovery of the crime, the arrest of suspects, and the charging of the suspects. Over half of the sources for crime news, according to Chermak (1994), are police and court officials (pp. 108, 111).

The result of the emphasis on crime news is that the public now relies on mass media for information about local conditions. Results from one panel indi-

Competition in Local TV News, by Angela Powers, Northern Illinois University

Television news is the number one source of news for Americans, yet its popularity has come under question as ratings decline. Stempel, Hargrove, and Bernt (2000) report that nationwide viewing of local TV news declined from 71% in 1995 to 59% in 1999 (p. 73). Some fear that viewing habits are changing and more people are switching to entertainment programming rather than watching news. Others believe that the proliferation of choices in the past decade has made all network television programs vulnerable to decreasing advertising revenues and increasing competition. What most scholars agree on is that the market structure of local television news is undergoing rapid change, resulting in a lack of equilibrium.

A television market includes a group of buyers (consumers and advertisers) and sellers (local television stations) engaged in terms of setting prices on advertising time and producing a news product. Variables that determine whether a monopoly, oligopoly, or competitive monopoly exist in a television market include number of competitors, as well as the stability of market shares and the level of product differentiation (Caves, 1987).

Local television news markets have traditionally been defined in terms of oligopoly theory where there are few sellers that cooperate in mutual interdependence and produce goods that are similar in many respects but have product differentiation (Litman, 1980). When a few hands controlled the local television industry, the stations were more dependent on each other and found it relatively easy to reach and maintain an agreement among them. For example, all stations in many markets aired news in similar day-parts, created similar advertising price structures, and covered similar news. However, this is no longer true in most markets, indicating a shift from oligopoly to competitive monopoly, where there are many sellers, and there is product differentiation.

With additional cable news networks, and different sources of distribution such as satellite systems and the telephone companies, the number of news options has increased. Bae (1999) analyzed competition among 24-hr cable news networks and found that new entrants to the market included Satellite News Channel (SNC), Microsoft and NBC (MSNBC), and Fox News Channel (FNC), among others. These cable networks compete with every other network for the viewing public, and they also compete with other closely substitutable news programs. In addition to cable, Collette and Litman (1997) examined the emergence of two new broadcast networks, United Paramount and Warner Brothers, which both produce news in local markets. These new networks survived formidable cost barriers because they aligned themselves with independent stations across the nation. In this way, they were able to compete with ABC-, CBS-, and NBC-affiliated stations. Baldwin, Barrett, and Bates (1992) studied both broadcast viewers and cable subscribers and compared consumption patterns of news. They found that if viewers were limited to one channel, 40% responded they would choose Cable News Network (CNN) for national and international news. However, CNN was not the news source of choice, as much as the broadcast news networks in any day-part. Although cable news services have grown, broadcast news was still found to be the dominant source of news.

Despite the strength of local network affiliates, a recent study of ratings in large, medium, and small markets found an increase in competition and a decrease in ratings since 1987. Overall, the number of broadcast television news competitors has increased by a range of one to four in most markets, excluding cable newscasts. In addition, market shares have decreased from 20 to 16. To combat this ratings decline, local broadcasters are creating a presence throughout the day by producing morning and afternoon feature news programs with news personalities similar to radio morning and afternoon talk shows. Adding news throughout the day is seen as the most viable way to improve overall ratings. In smaller markets, the stations that were rated number 1 at 10 p.m. offered the most news throughout the day. In large markets, the stations ranked third in the market offered the most news. Although market leaders and trailers were more likely to program the most news, all stations have increased their news visibility over the past decade in an effort to compete. As such, local broadcast news can be increasingly described as departing from its oligopolistic past where market shares were high and competition was limited to three stations (Powers, 2001).

This product differentiation behavior of adding news has benefitted viewers because news is now available throughout the day. This also appeals to younger viewers who are less likely to be available at traditional newscast times. But adding more news comes at a cost. More reporters are required to create quality news throughout the day. However, the burden of more news is often heaped onto the shoulders of already-harried news reporters. Furthermore, the additional newscasts are often a rehash of earlier newscasts. Although the goal is to attract viewers, it is most often tempered by the goal to keep costs down. Media analysts have stated that in a mature economy with a business that is equally mature, news organizations will find it more difficult to remain profitable (McClellan, 1998).

BOX 2.3

cated that, "Ninety-five percent of the answers rated the mass media as the primary source" (Graber, 1980, p. 49). Graber (1980) saw news as a matter of information process in which theories such as agenda setting have only limited value. Graber (1980) suggested that crime news fits more closely into a "modulator" model of audience effects:

> Proponents of the modulator model argue that effects of the media on the audience are modulated by the sensitivity of the audience to a particular issue and by the background and demographic characteristics and experiences of individual audience members. Modulation enhances or decreases media impact, depending on the salience of a specific issue to an individual. (Graber, 1980, p. 121)

Altheide (1985) contended that most people are not interested in issues but are concerned with personal problems. He asserted that a report about conflict at a distance will concern the audience only to the extent that it affects them personally. "By the same token, 'crime in the streets' is salient to those persons who either know little about the actual incidence and nature of criminal behavior and/or have been previously victimized" (pp. 171–172). For local television news crime coverage to be appealing to those with no personal experience or interest, there must be a dramatic and emotional portrayal: "The need for effective video and sound bites—as well as the need to appeal to a mass audience—also lead local television news to search for news stories and approaches to the news that stress emotion and drama" (Kaniss, 1991, p. 109). Kaniss (1991) found that coverage of "occurrences"—isolated crimes, accidents and fires—accounted for nearly one third of local television news-time. This was about the same amount of time afforded government stories (p. 114). "Government stories were also consistently lower in the story order and reduced in time between 6 and 11 o'clock, supplanted by news of crimes, fires, and accidents" (pp. 118–119).

Koch (1990) theorized that the process of gatekeeping and news making, seen through a social context, means that news is socially-constructed myth based on news values rather than objective truth. "This inherent value system—the mythic language—describes a reportorial perspective in which events consistently are mediated through a single complex of cultural values" (p. 28). Koch (p. 50) identified four rules that help explain why an event may be worthy of news coverage:

1. *Cultural rules* help define events as newsworthy.
2. *Social rules* assign a weight to specific stories.
3. *Geographic rules* set boundaries which limit the distance a news organization might travel.
4. *Temporal rules* govern the time frame within which an event occurs.

In the case of local television news coverage of crime, cultural rules would guide an assignment editor's decisions about covering an event. Social rules would guide a producer in the placement of the story within a newscast. Geographic rules guide various newsroom employees to make decisions about the allocation of scarce resources—namely, time and money. Temporal rules deal with newscast deadlines and the ability to produce a live shot, sound bite, or package in time for a particular newscast. It is fair to say that these four rules interact in complex ways to produce what is seen on the broadcast. For example, if police respond to a report that there is a disturbance at a local high school an hour before a station's midday newscast, it is possible that cultural rules will dictate coverage of the event. If it turns out that there has been a shooting and there are known victims, then social rules will suggest this is a lead story. At this point, geography interacts with time considerations. It will take a certain amount of time to get a live truck and crew to the scene, and this depends on how far the station is located from the school. If possible, the newsroom goal will be to have video, live coverage, and interviews by air time. Whatever the station manages to get on the air during the broadcast, according to Koch (1990), will tend to be treated by the audience as an objective "truth" about what is happening. In this way, the local station participates in placing facts of the event within a particular context for viewers:

> Local news, like other forms of news, is driven by the need for large audiences. Issues that are attention-getting that generate compelling visual images, and that fit the fast-paced nature of broadcast news are especially likely to attract coverage. Crime is just such an issue ... local news coverage of crime ... is framed in ways that have far-reaching consequences for the ways in which people think about the issue of crime. (Iyengar, 1997, p. 215)

Once the basic facts of any breaking news story are determined by local television news stations, the focus shifts to an attempt to explain why the event took place. Surette (1998) suggested that media images locate the causes of crime in individuals and support society's approach to dealing with criminals: "These messages translate into support for law-and-order policies and existing criminal justice agencies" (p. 82). Police department spokespersons, public information officers, and other authorities become the experts in setting the limits of which facts are viewed as important. So, although early in a breaking news story eyewitness accounts are important, norms of accuracy and the need to explain leads to a later emphasis on official sources. Those sources may have a calming effect on the public as the event evolves from moments of chaos toward a return to normalcy. Each event, however, has its own time frame. In this sense, local television news must yield to the conditions at the same time as it helps to frame the meaning of newsworthy events.

CHAPTER SUMMARY

This chapter focused on mass media research as it relates to crime news on local television. Theories and concepts about news were utilized to help explain why crime stories play such a prominent role in local newscasts. It can be said that crimes are central to local television news gathering, and the result is that audience members see a lot of crime news coverage.

The dominant theories in research about crime news coverage are social construction of reality, cultivation, and cultural meaning making. Social construction of reality in local television news emphasizes close-up views that create a sense of familiarity with distant people and places, live event coverage that give viewers a sense of participation, pictures that seem authentic to viewers, and coverage that may provide a more complete picture of the event than available from other media. The cultivation hypothesis is that "heavy" viewers will be more likely to perceive the real world in ways that reflect the most stable and recurrent patterns of portrayals in the television world. From a cultural meaning making perspective, there are two communication models: transmission and cultural. The transmission model is the traditional linear view of communication that focuses on how media messages are sent to the audience. In contrast, the cultural model emphasizes shared meanings and spaces. The process of gatekeeping and news making, seen through a social context, means that news is socially-constructed and based on news values. In the next chapter, the business of local television news and its use of crime within newscasts will be examined. Crime news will be viewed as a ratings builder for local television stations. The use of gatekeeping rituals by local news producers that emphasize breaking news and live coverage will be explored.

DISCUSSION QUESTIONS

1. Do you believe that local television stations in your city provide an objective portrayal of crime or a subjective construction of events?
2. Why do you think that some people are loyal viewers of one channel's local newscast, while others channel surf? What type of viewer are you? Why?
3. If you were a local television news director, what limits would you set on the amount and type of graphic video your newscast would air? Why?
4. Do you agree or disagree that local television newscasts provide audience members with interpretations of events in the community? What role does local television news play in how people make sense about the nature of crime in their community?
5. In your opinion, do local television news producers make decisions to cover crime based on business or ratings pressures? What other factors might play a role in their decision-making processes?

3

Crime News
as Ratings Builders

"The local television news, with its heavy crime component, has eclipsed national news, which carries more serious political stories and less crime, in the battle for high audience ratings."

—Doris Graber, political scientist (1993, p. 332).

Crime news, by one estimate, accounts for about 14% of local news coverage, and the lion's share of that coverage focuses on sensational events (Graber, 1993). Graber (1993) argued that the public, despite public complaints, has a hunger for exciting crime news.

This chapter builds on the previous chapter and explains why TV news utilizes crime coverage in the pursuit of viewers by drawing from survey research and content analysis. In 1999, news directors and assignment editors from local television stations around the nation were surveyed. The national random sample asked their opinions regarding their station's crime news coverage and other issues. This followed a 1997 survey of local television news producers. During the fall of 1999, a 1-week sample of selected late evening newscasts from around the country were recorded and examined for evidence of crime coverage. The overall purpose of the analysis was to update Graber's (1980) analysis, focus on local television news, and attempt to place crime coverage within the larger context of news decision making and the television business.

THE BUSINESS OF LOCAL TV NEWS

Mass media organizations are like any other business: they exist to make money. As such, the people at the top of these organizations are involved in the management process. "[M]anagement consists of (1) the ability to supervise and motivate employees and (2) the ability to operate facilities and resources in a cost-effective (profitable) manner" (Sherman, 1995, p. 22). To do this is often difficult:

> Several demands—for information and entertainment by the audience, for profits by stockholders and owners, and for access for advertisers—place managers of electronic media facilities in a challenging position as they try to serve the needs of the market along with the needs of the marketplace. (Albarran, 1997, p. 4)

Any study of local television news today comes within an emerging context of commercialism and marketing. The line between advertising and news has blurred in recent years.

The historical heart and soul of the electronic communication field is local and national broadcasting. Broadcast managers, as you might expect, are the bosses wielding the most power at a station. Studies of media management (Albarran, 1997; Goedkoop, 1988; Jacobs, 1990; Sherman, 1995) reveal that there are several key people within any local broadcast station such as the general manager,

---

National Public Radio's Brooke Gladstone has reported on the relation between advertising and news at WBAL–TV, Channel 11, in Baltimore. The Mercy Medical Center had an ongoing relation with the television station to report on women's health issues, such as breast and ovarian cancer: "Their experts are appearing on the news not necessarily because they know the most about the subject, but because they bought the time for their experts to be on the news, and that's not told to the viewer in any way," said Paul Rayburn of *BusinessWeek* magazine. WBAL's President and General Manager Bill Fein rejected the conclusion that the medical center's advertising budget influences news decision making: "Mercy's doctors, in consultation with our news, were used with total editorial control belonging to WBAL–TV to provide information to our viewers."

Some medical experts estimate that deals between local television stations and outside organizations range from $20,000 to $100,000 in revenues. This money can buy access to assignment editors and influence selection of story ideas and sources. Said Steve Bryant of the Association of American Medical Colleges, "You expect news judgment to prevail and I think people would be surprised to know that sometimes there is a sort of nodding and winking relationship between a sponsor of one of these education initiatives and appearance within the newscast." However, Fein challenged the notion that sponsors buy access: "They buy advertising time. Separately from that, they help us provide information to our viewers."

Source: Brook Gladstone, "Hospitals That Pay Local Television Stations To Feature Their Doctors In News Reports And Whether It's Good For Patients Or The Public's Trust In Television," Morning Edition, National Public Radio, March 28, 2000.

BOX 3.1   The Selling of Local Television News.

the program director, the sales manager, and the news director. The general manager is important because that person has overall responsibility for the station's profitability and community relations. In most cases, the general manager of a television station is not at the top of the organizational chart—the manager usually reports to an owner or corporate office. There are other internal forces within any media organization affecting management. For example, a broadcast manager must live within a budget usually planned on a yearly basis. It is fair to say there are different management styles. Some managers

- Are better communicators than others because they have strong interpersonal skills.
- Offer their department heads more freedom to make decisions.
- Have more of a head for budgeting than others.
- Are better salespeople than others, and are better at representing their station in the community.
- Realize the significance of local news.

Beyond those internal factors which a manager may face daily, there are pressures outside the broadcast organization. Some of these are station ratings, market competition, government regulation, financial constraints, programming trends in the industry, and new technologies. Broadcasting is considered a profession in which individuals first aspire to enter the field, and then usually seek training. Often this training begins in the classroom. Beyond college course work, most broadcasters obtain experience in the industry—whether it is in news, programming, production, or sales departments—before being promoted into management. There has been a trend among general managers to view news directors as future general managers (Stone, 1986). Quarderer and Stone (1989a, 1989b) found that news directors and general managers share similar beliefs about news and bottom-line profitability. In a national survey of news directors, 49.5% of men and 22.2% of women set a long-term goal of being promoted in management (Burks & Stone, 1993).

The broader sociology of work (Blum, Roman, & Tootle, 1988), and its professional or occupational attitudes (Super, 1980), has not found its way into research on broadcast managers. One such model, for example, sees maturation as a series of stages: prework socialization, entry into the labor force, socialization in the job, and job change. The focus on occupation—rather than the usual organizational emphasis (Gitlin, 1980)—means that the research focus changes from an examination of the dynamics of what goes on inside stations to an analysis of broadcast managers across stations. Using this model, news managers may be compared to their general managers. "News directors, while not as pro-business as general managers, show some support for business freedoms" (Lipschultz & Hilt, 1993, p. 524).

In the past 25 years, broadcast stations have experienced a dramatic shift in terms of gender. Large numbers of women have been hired and promoted at local broadcast stations. For example, a majority of the television news managers (producers, assignment editors, and news directors) in Omaha, NE (75th largest market), are now women, and one of the stations hired the market's first female general manager. In the past decade, increasing numbers of women have been promoted into management positions. The changes have also given rise to new issues, such as the concern over sexual harassment in the workplace. Similarly, age discrimination complaints by some broadcast employees have surfaced. Aging has also become important as the average age of the broadcast audience increases.

General Managers and News Directors

Historically, it has been assumed that the role of a broadcast general manager varies greatly from that of a news director. Although the business-oriented general manager is responsible for station adherence to FCC regulations, the news director is seen as overseeing specific programming (Sherman, 1995).

One might assume that if a general manager comes from a sales, promotion, or programming background, and a news director from a journalism background, there might be tension between financial and journalistic issues. However, Lipschultz and Hilt (1993) found that general managers supported a

---

Modern News Management. Jim Ogle, Vice President for News, WKYT–TV, Lexington, Kentucky

The modern news manager must understand that good journalism is good business. "That's not as trite as it sounds. I believe that 'good journalism' is reporting that doesn't just point fingers, but looks for alternatives. It doesn't just expose problems, but looks for solutions. It helps people connect and cope. It is a good citizen of its community," Ogle said. "It cares. It must understand that a community has values and mores and reflects those back to the general public."

The typical manager experiences many communities while employed by media groups or corporations. For example, Jim Ogle began his professional life while a student at the University of Missouri in the early 1980s. After graduation, he moved to Asheville, NC, to work as an executive producer at WLOS–TV. From there he became a news director at KTVN–TV, Reno, NV, and then on to WGHP–TV, High Point, NC. By the late 1980s, Ogle served as managing editor at WTVJ–TV, NBC's owned-and-operated station in Miami, FL. He moved to his current Lexington, KY, job in 1994.

Under Ogle's tenure, 27 NewsFirst expanded its news product by adding an afternoon information magazine, a 5 p.m. newscast, a 10 p.m. newscast on the local Fox affiliate (WDKY–TV), and an expanded sports program. WKYT–TV, in the 71st largest market, has dominated ratings in the Lexington television market for more than 25 years. Its average newscast has more viewers than its two competitors combined.

BOX 3.2

strong news department when it was seen as good for business, and news directors showed some support for probusiness attitudes.

Late Evening News Producers

Although general managers set overall station policy, and news directors set newsroom policy, producers are responsible for the final content of television newscasts: "Once a decision has been made on which newscast a story will be placed, the reporter will do most of his or her communicating with the producer on questions of story focus, length, etc." (Goedkoop, 1988, p. 72). As much as half of the overall news content is written not by reporters but by producers. Producers must work in an increasingly competitive environment in which market shares for late evening newscasts have declined dramatically since the 1980s (Jacobs, 1990).

Assignment Editors

"The assignment editor's job is to cover everything that happens, a responsibility some broadcasters consider to be the toughest job in the news department" (Shook, 1996, p. 247):

> The assignment editor assigns crews, answers the phone, follows breaking news, checks the wire machines, monitors police–fire–sheriff's radios, sorts and reads the mail, studies local newspapers, monitors broadcast news competitors, reads scripts of previous newscasts, keeps a news file, develops story ideas and sometimes helps write the stories, follows developing stories, makes and adjusts schedules, helps organize the newsroom, and negotiates conflicts between staff members. (p. 248)

The assignment editor typically arrives early in the morning to plan the day's coverage. He or she may be involved in several assignment meetings with reporters, producers, anchors, and others throughout the day. An assignment editor faces a long day at work. "Then, in the late afternoon, he or she begins to plan the coverage and probable stories for the next day while still looking over his or her shoulder to see if there are any immediate problems that might need attention" (Goedkoop, 1988, p. 30). The assignment editor may be on the job into the early evening. "The assignment editor's position requires precise attention to detail, as well as the ability to plan and to be flexible" (Goedkeep, 1988, pp. 30–31).

Organizations, Professional Roles, and Job Satisfaction

Local television news workers are driven by at least two sets of values, those of the broadcast news profession, and those of their organization. Pollard (1995) sug-

A former local television news assignment editor explains the assignment process. After the assignment editor checks the news file, reads the mail, examines competing media, makes telephone calls, and scans the news wires, decisions need to be made. News managers judge which stories need to be covered. Once a news story is selected, the attention turns to how to cover it:

1. Voice overs—usually only send photographer.
2. Voice over sound on tape—sometimes send reporter,
3. Packages—most important or interesting stories.
4. Set pieces—very important or hard to visualize stories.
5. Live—late breaking or ongoing stories.
6. Live satellite—for far away stories.

Given the breadth of work required of assignment editors, one might reasonably ask the following: "Why would anybody want to do this job?" Debra Westhues, Assignment Editor at KCTV in Kansas City, MO, offered the following opinions:

• Assignment Editors experience the excitement of working in the news business without a lot of the physical unpleasantness: unbearable heat or cold, driving rain and floods, and daily dose of dead bodies.
• Assignment Editors are able to deal with all of the elements involved with the business instead of only one.
• Assignment Editors find better job availability.

Source: Debra Westhues, Assignment Editor, KCTV, Kansas City, KS, 1988.

BOX 3.3 An Assignment Editor Describes Local TV Story Decisions.

gested that the organizational desire to be profitable produces "tension and potential conflict" with the professional desire for excellence (p. 682). Local TV news has historically been motivated by a desire to serve community needs (Slattery, Hakanen, & Doremus, 1996). Scholars have concluded that professional "ideology ... is the unconscious outcome of business structure, bureaucratic routine, and organizational practice" (Wu, Weaver, & Johnson, 1996, p. 535).

Professionalism in broadcasting is related to the concept of job satisfaction because the "dual control centers" of the profession and the organization lead to attempts to reduce tension. "To thwart conflict, organizations may attempt to absorb practitioners by offering socioeconomic rewards such as job titles, or pay increases to those who will place organizational interests, such as competitiveness or profitability, ahead of professional concerns, such as full use of professional knowledge and skills or collegiality" (Pollard & Johansen, 1998, p. 357).

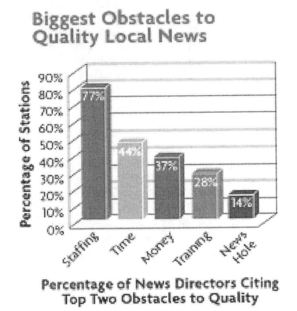

Biggest Obstacles to Quality Local News

Percentage of News Directors Citing Top Two Obstacles to Quality

FIG. 3.1 Project for excellence in journalism responses by news directors to quality concerns. *Source:* Project for Excellence in Journalism, 1999, used with permission.

TOP FIVE LOCAL NEWS TOPICS IN 2000

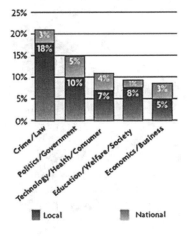

FIG. 3.2

TABLE 3.1

Agreement With Late Evening Newscast Decision Statements

"Do You Agree or Disagree With the Following Statements About Your Late Evening Newscast?" (N = 71)

	Percentage Agree or Strongly Agree	Percentage Neutral	Percentage Disagree or Strongly Disagree
Agree			
We often lead with local news (4.75).	**95.8**	4.2	0.0
I know what the news director wants in the newscast (4.17).	**88.4**	8.7	2.8
We lead with the most important news story, wherever it occurs (4.04).	**73.3**	19.7	7.0
I tell reporters what I want (4.00).	**82.9**	12.9	4.3
I look for dramatic video in deciding which stories to air (3.62).	**62.0**	28.2	9.9
The executive producer regularly decides what leads (3.23).	**50.7**	20.3	28.9
Mixed			
We often lead with crime news (3.17).	42.3	22.5	35.2
Our audience research guides what we broadcast (3.07).	45.7	27.1	27.1
We consider our primetime lead-in show in deciding what to air (2.92).	32.4	32.4	35.2

(continued on next page)

TABLE 3.1 *(continued)*

Agreement With Late Evening Newscast Decision Statements

"Do You Agree or Disagree With the Following Statements About Your Late Evening Newscast?" (N = 71)

	Percentage Agree or Strongly Agree	Percentage Neutral	Percentage Disagree or Strongly Disagree
Disagree			
The assignment editor regularly decides what leads (2.41).	13.0	27.5	**59.4**
Our news consultant guides what we broadcast (2.37).	21.5	24.3	**54.3**
We often lead with national news (2.24).	10.0	25.7	**64.3**

Note. The 5-point Likert-type scale items were coded for the averages in parentheses as the following: 1 = *strongly disagree*, 2 = *disagree*, 3 = *neutral*, 4 = *agree*, and 5 = *strongly agree*. The percentages in the table were collapsed to reflect disagreement and agreement. Bold indicates numbers over 50%.

This may result in the organization adopting formalized standards for work and centralized "hierarchical authority" (Pollard & Johansen, 1998, p. 358).

In the case of local television news, job satisfaction has been related to news department goals and relationship–orientation of news directors (Powers & Lacy, 1992). The more a news director is able to use communication skills to lead newsroom employees toward a common set of goals, the more likely it is for employees to have job satisfaction. Job satisfaction has also been related to the impact of newsroom policy changes. In general, if employees see quality improving, their job satisfaction levels are likely to be higher (Stamm & Underwood, 1993). Other factors which could raise employee job satisfaction levels are advancement, recognition, and feedback from coworkers and supervisors (Fox, 1997). At the same time, low pay and lack of job security may be "dissatisfiers" (p. 30). Within local television stations, there is an organizational context to job satisfaction. Factors such as management conflicts, workloads and deadlines, job security, and coworker relations have been linked to stress management (Vampola & Hilt, 1996).

A local television news organization may be able to improve job satisfaction by allowing for "meaningful employee participation in decisions, and limited reliance on hierarchical authority and rule enforcement" (Pollard, 1995, p. 683).

TABLE 3.2

Local News Statements

"Do You Agree or Disagree With the Following Statements Concerning Your Station's Coverage of Local Crime News?" (N = 71)

	Percentage Agree or Strongly Agree	Percentage Neutral	Percentage Disagree or Strongly Disagree
Agree			
Spot news from the scene of natural disasters, including severe weather, deserves live coverage (4.47).	95.8	2.9	1.4
Spot news from the scene of fatal shootings, police chases, standoffs, and so forth, deserves live coverage (3.61).	58.6	27.1	14.3
Dramatic video is a factor in determining whether a story should be broadcast (3.59).	68.6	15.7	15.7
Loss of life a factor in determining whether a story should be broadcast (3.49).	62.9	14.3	22.9
Mixed			
Spot news from the scene of fatal accidents and fires deserves live coverage (3.39).	44.3	38.6	17.2
Disagree			
Graphic video, such as body bags and blood on the pavement, should be shown in spot news stories (2.03).	8.5	26.8	64.7

Note. The 5-point Likert-type scale items were coded for the averages in parentheses as the following: 1 = strongly disagree, 2 = disagree, 3 = neutral, 4 = agree, and 5 = strongly agree. The percentages in the table were collapsed to reflect disagreement and agreement. Bold indicates numbers larger than 50%.

TABLE 3.3

Comparison of Average Agreement With Late Evening
Newscast Decision Statements

*"Do You Agree or Disagree With the Following Statements
About Your Late Evening Newscast?"*

	News Directors (N = 35)	Assignment Editors (N = 36)	News Producers (N = 35)
Agree			
We often lead with local news (4.74).	4.74	4.75	4.71
We lead with the most important news story, wherever it occurs (4.10).	4.00	4.08	4.21
I know what the news director wants in the newscast (4.09).	4.33	4.03	3.91
I tell reporters what I want (4.03).	3.91	4.08	4.09
I look for dramatic video in deciding which stories to air (3.72).	**3.31**	3.92	3.94
We often lead with crime news (3.22).	3.06	3.28	3.32
Mixed			
The executive producer regularly decides what leads (3.13).	2.94	3.50	2.91
Our audience research guides what we broadcast (3.09).	**2.63**	**3.51**	3.11
We consider our primetime lead-in show in deciding what to air (2.82).	2.51	**3.31**	2.62
Disagree			
Our news consultant guides what we broadcast (2.38).	**1.91**	**2.83**	2.41
We often lead with national news (2.29).	2.26	2.22	2.39
The assignment editor regularly decides what leads (2.27).	2.32	2.49	2.00

Note. The 5-point Likert-type scale items were coded for the averages in parentheses as the following: 1 = *strongly disagree*, 2 = *disagree*, 3 = *neutral*, 4 = *agree*, and 5 = *strongly agree*. The percentages in the table were collapsed to reflect disagreement and agreement. Bolded means are statistically significant subgroups based on a post hoc Scheffe test. Producer data are from a separate 1997 survey in which 35 respondents were randomly selected from 87 respondents in that study.

However, financial decision making usually involves annual budget meetings that are limited to department heads, such as the news director. Although a general manager's budget attempts to forecast financial success of the station, there also must be "budgetary flexibility" (Albarran, 1997, p. 54). Budgeting and bottom-line issues may be thought of as management "tasks" that affect how subordinates view their managers' leadership skills (Powers & Lacy, 1992, p. 8).

A national study of local television news directors listed the five biggest obstacles to presenting a quality newscast. Four of the five concerns raised by the news directors relate directly to the bottom line.

The responses suggest that the news managers define quality in terms of the number of stories in a newscast rather than the content of those stories. The coverage of spot news crime stories is economically convenient when compared with issue-oriented in-depth coverage. It is possible to do a live shot on a breaking crime story with two or three field employees, without much planning time, and for not much added expense. Reporters, photographers and newsroom staffers are already trained to handle breaking spot news, and they have little difficulty fitting it into existing news holes.

Views of News Managers Concerning Crime Coverage

The results from a national survey of news directors and assignment editors suggest that local news is most important in decision making about late evening news broadcasts. Although the late evening news happens hours after the nightly network news broadcast, national news takes a back seat to local stories. The exception is when a national news story is deemed by news management as most important within the context of everything happening that evening. It appears that the presence of dramatic video in a story is a deciding factor in determining whether a local or national news story rises to the top of importance. Drama, important in entertainment programming (Reith, 1999), may also be central to local news programming as a way to attract viewers. News directors and assignment editors were less certain about the role crime news plays in the decision process about lead stories. Although 42.3% said they often lead with crime news, 22.5% were neutral, and 35.2% disagreed. There appeared to be a subgroup of stations more interested in crime news and audience research. A majority of all respondents disagreed that news consultants influence the process, or that national news stories are a frequent lead.

A 1999 national survey of local television news directors and assignment editors found strong agreement that local coverage was most important in deciding late evening news leads. The news managers were split on the importance of crime news, but 42.3% agreed that they often lead with crime stories.

The news directors and assignment editors agreed that spot news and dramatic video were the key components in crime coverage, but they disagreed that graphic video should be shown.

The 1999 data from news directors and assignment editors were compared to 1997 survey data from local television late evening news producers. Among agreement statements, the only statistically significant difference between groups was that news directors were less likely to agree that dramatic video should be considered when deciding on the airing of a story.

Assignment editors were in significantly higher agreement than news directors that audience research and primetime programming lead-ins to the late evening newscast were considerations in deciding which stories to air. Beyond this, news directors were the only group in strong disagreement that consultants guide what is broadcast.

There were demographic differences between the three occupations. The typical news director in the study was a 39-year-old White (94.3%) man (65.7%), who had a college degree (41.4 %), had worked in the news business for 17 years, and earned in excess of $35,000 (70.6%).

The typical assignment editor was a 39-year-old White (97.2%) man (72.2%), who had a college degree (80.6%), had worked in the news business for 11 years, and earned $35,000 or less (62.9%).

The typical late evening news producer was a 34-year-old White (94.3%) woman (57.1%), who had a college degree (88.6%), had worked in the news business for 7 years, and earned $35,000 or less (69.7%).

The following study examined how newsroom decisions translate into crime news coverage.

The Content of Local Television News, by Christine R. Mixan

Local television news coverage of crime was studied. A "purposive" sample (Babbie, 1998, p. 195) of small, medium, and large television markets from around the country were selected for content analysis. Television professionals, academics, and others in key markets were contacted by e-mail and telephone to participate in taping late evening newscasts during the week of October 11 to 15, 1999. A network-affiliated station (ABC, CBS, FOX, and NBC) was randomly assigned to each person who agreed to tape. The goal was to obtain a wide range of markets and affiliates across the United States. In the end, 17 respondents sent usable tapes for analysis. The tapes contained five newscasts from each night of the week (Monday–Friday) sampled, for a total of 82 newscasts (one tape did not contain all five broadcasts).

The market list reflects the availability of people willing to tape. Unfortunately, there are no stations from the Northeast or Northwest, only three stations are NBC affiliates whereas six are FOX stations, and 11 of 17 stations are from the top half of the Nielsen media research markets (Broadcasting & Cable Yearbook, 1999).

In this study, crime was defined as the following: a known or alleged violation or serious offense of the public law. The types of crimes were coded in the following categories: murder, assault, rape, drugs, theft, fraud, child abuse, sexual harassment, white collar, arson, threats, kidnapping, and other (Klite & Bardwell, 1997). A post hoc check using Holsti's (1969) formula revealed intercoder reliability of .857.

A total of 138 crime stories aired in the first segment of the newscasts, and 31.0% were presented as either packages or a combination of a live or package report (14.4% package; 16.6% live or package). The percentage of crime stories as voice-overs was the greatest (37.6%), followed by voice-over and sound-on-tape (22.4%), readers (5.0%), and live reports (4.0%). The analysis was limited to the first segment of each broadcast.

Twenty-seven out of the 82 lead stories (32.9%) were crime-related. This percentage was higher than for any other type of story: 17.1% concerned the courts; 9.8% were government or public affairs stories; 9.8% were weather or natural disasters; 8.5% were human interest stories; 7.3% were accidents; 6.1% were education issues; 2.4% were environmental issues; 1.2% were political coverage; 1.2% were health issues, and there were no lead stories about public moral problems or business and the economy. An additional 3.7% of "other" stories fit none of the established categories. Among lead crime stories, assaults and a jail escape (other category) received the most coverage.

Only two types of crimes were recorded in the "other" section: two stories about criminals violating court orders, and six stories about a criminal who escaped while he was being transported from one jail to another.

Creswell's (1994) qualitative research techniques were used to study common images and language found in the crime stories. The images that appeared most included "scene of the crime" footage, shots of crowds and media gathered at the crime scene, courtroom footage, police searching for suspects and investigating the crime scene. Other images not shown as frequently, but still regularly appearing in the newscasts, were the following: home videos of the victim, still photos of the murdered victim, still photos of the criminal, police sketches of the criminal, damaged police cars, damaged criminals' cars, and paramedics transporting injured people.

There was only one story that aired video of the crime while it was actually being committed. This involved a man who claimed he had explosives strapped to his body. The camera showed us the man as he positioned himself against a downtown monument yelling to the gathered crowd and the police that he had explosives. The camera stayed on the man until he threw his hands up and surrendered.

There was also only one story that aired video of police actually arresting a criminal. The camera stayed on the criminal as he struggled with police on the way to the police cruiser.

Photographers used several interesting techniques while videotaping the footage for their stories. As one might expect, close-ups were often used when showing a person's face, especially the victim of a crime or the friends and family of the victim. In addition, zooming the camera quickly outward or inward on an object seemed to convey a dramatic effect in the story. Also, videotaping an object out-of-focus and then turning the lens to bring it into focus seemed to convey a similar dramatic effect. Finally, if a station wanted to reenact a dramatic event, the photographer would retrace the steps of the victim or criminal, walking while videotaping the supposed path the criminal or victim took. For example, one reporter told a story about a woman who had been abducted, raped, and then had to run up the hill to a nearby house in the middle of a field to get help. To convey this dramatic event to the viewers at home, the photographer recreated the scene as if she were running up the hill and through the field to get to the house.

Several common language devices emerged. First, many adjectives and descriptive terms were used such as the following: "a dangerous chase," "dramatic car crash," "violent takeover robbery," "terrifying ordeal," and "heartbreaking call." Other adjectives and words commonly used were "nightmare," "tragedy," "brutal," "terror," "desperate," "terrorized," and "disturbing."

Additionally, when a more colorful term or word could be substituted for an objective term, it was. For example, one station did a string of stories throughout the week on the search for convicted killer Kyle Bell. He escaped while being transported from one prison to another. Instead of saying, "State police are searching for Kyle Bell," the anchor read, "State police are on a manhunt tonight."

Furthermore, many reporters used a narrative open with words or phrases that contrasted with each other. For example, on telling her audience that police caught a kidnapper, one reporter stated, "In the heavy brush alongside the calm river lies the metro's most wanted man."

Another reporter went to great lengths to set the scene of a terrible incident happening in a peaceful neighborhood. One can see that the following narrative again accentuates the contrasting device mentioned earlier:

> Sixteen houses make up this neighborhood; a close community where next weekend neighbors will gather for the annual fall festival. This evening, they gathered in concern, as word quickly spread that a teenager had been shot inside this home. Police carried out bags full of evidence. Neighbors were full of questions. The Monday afternoon quiet was pierced with screams. Apparently, one teen shot another teen with a 9-millimeter automatic pistol. Three hours after the screams and the gunshot rang out, police took away the crime scene tape, but not the questions.

Reporters and anchors used active tense in their writing. This came in the form of phrases such as the following: "this just in," "we have breaking news," and "police tell us." Several stations used consultant phrases such as "tonight's big story," "this just in," and "breaking news" to convey a sense of urgency or importance. This was often followed by graphic details of the crime: "... her clothes were ripped off, she was repeatedly raped, with both her hands and feet bound, and then left here...." The reporter made a gesture of her hands being bound as she gave her stand-up.

A final characteristic emerging from the language in local lead TV crime stories came from the selection of sound bites. Many of the sources made claims about some element of the story being covered, but gave no basis or evidence for those claims. For example, one police officer was speaking about a criminal who escaped from prison when he said, "It's just a matter of time before he hurts someone else." Daly and Chasteen (1996) found that in 90% of the crime stories they studied, sources offered no evidence to support their claims. In fairness to these sources, however, perhaps the evidence they gave was edited out of the story.

BOX 3.4

TABLE 3.4

Local Television Newscasts Studied in 1999

Station	City, State	Network Affiliation	Market Size
KTTV–11	Los Angeles, CA	FOX	2
WLS–7	Chicago, IL	ABC	3
KXAS–5	Dallas–Fort Worth, TX	NBC	7
KSTP–5	Minneapolis, MN	ABC	15
WSVN–7	Miami, FL	FOX	16
KCNC–4	Denver, CO	CBS	18
KMBC–9	Kansas City, MO	ABC	33
WBNS–10	Columbus, OH	CBS	34*
KOAT–TV7	Albuquerque, NM	ABC	49
WKYT–27	Lexington, KY	CBS	67
KPTM–42	Omaha, NE	FOX	73
KAME–2	Reno, NV	FOX	108
WPDE–15	Florence–Myrtle Beach, SC	ABC	112
KXJB–4	Fargo, ND	CBS	115
KIVI–6	Boise–Nampa, ID	ABC	125
KDLH–3	Duluth, MN	CBS	135
WTOK–11	Meridian, MS	ABC	183

*WCMH–4, the NBC affiliate, was also viewed in this market.

A WEEK IN THE LIFE OF TELEVISION NEWS

The week of October 11 to 15, 1999, offered an interesting contrast between the decisions made by network news producers and those of the local stations under study. A day-by-day review of transcripts and tapes will be treated as a

TABLE 3.5

Type of Lead Crime Stories in Local TV News

Crime type	N	Percentage
Assault	7	21.2
Theft	4	12.1
Kidnapping	3	9.1
Murder	2	6.1
Rape	2	6.1
Threats	2	6.1
Arson	2	6.1
Drugs	1	3.0
Fraud	1	3.0
Child abuse	1	3.0
White collar	0	0.0
Other (jail escape, court order violation)	8	24.2
	33[*]	100.0

Note. [*]Within crime-related stories, there were six stories where more than one type of crime was mentioned. For example, one of the stories reported on both murder and rape. So, although there were 27 crime-related stories, there were 33 crimes mentioned in those stories.

snapshot of television crime coverage in the United States. Only by comparing station coverage across the nation on the same day can one see the similarities and differences in news selection, emphasis, and presentation. Local TV news broadcasts often differ sharply from national network news in their judgments about what is most important to viewers. The local stations appear to believe that viewers are anxious to hear and see about sensational and dramatic events. Often, these stories seem to crowd out coverage of significant national and international public affairs news. Crime is one of the types of stories. Other types include severe weather, unexpected news about well-known people, and natural disasters. At the same time, unique local events often lead a station to make different decisions than their peers in other markets. The desire to be lo-

KTTV, Fox 11. Los Angeles: Mar Vista rape story, reporter live from the scene.

cal and regional above all other considerations means that there is no national standard on any given evening.

Monday, October 11, 1999

On Monday, the four television networks studied here (ABC, CBS, CNN, and NBC) featured substantive national and international stories on their nightly news broadcasts. Two (ABC and CNN) of the four networks led with floods in Mexico, a story given prominent play by only one of the local stations, the ABC affiliate in Chicago. CBS led with the Matthew Shepard murder trial in Wyoming. NBC led with the claim that Iraqi terrorism introduced the West Nile virus to New York. Three of the four networks (ABC, CBS, and NBC) featured the West Nile story. All four networks gave prominent play (the third story on ABC, CBS, and NBC, and the fourth on CNN) to a story about President Clinton's letter to the United States Senate urging postponement on the ratification vote for the nuclear test ban treaty—a story given little play on the local stations under study.

KMBC, ABC 9, Kansas City fatal car crash, hit by police car running without lights and siren.

WTOK–TV, Meridian, MS.   This small market station came out of ABC's Monday Night football with the following bump: "A dangerous chase in Meridian has left one law enforcement officer hurt." The suspect was shown being led away in handcuffs. The anchor said the chase started as a robbery, and a reporter package followed. The reporter stood in front of a shoe store where viewers were told the suspect had shown a gun, taken three pairs of shoes, and $100. Police quickly began a chase to a nearby Interstate highway. A highway trooper involved in the chase was interviewed. Several damaged police cars were shown, as well as the arrest scene along the Interstate. The reporter said the man was traveling at speeds of more than 100 miles per hr. The station showed the suspect restrained inside a cruiser, and the reporter noted that the suspect had resisted arrest.

KTTV–TV, Los Angeles, CA.   In Los Angeles, the Fox affiliate told viewers, "Two sexual assaults in just four days have left the Mar Vista neighborhood stunned and on alert tonight." The station used a double box with the anchor and reporter live at the scene, and titled it "RAPIST SEARCH." The reporter introduced a package:

> … It is not the first time that this has happened in this neighborhood. It is the kind of crime that tends to happen more often when the weather is warm and people leave their windows open at night. A little before 3 this morning, just up the street …, the attacker simply pulled the screen off a window to get inside his victim's home.…

The package began with a sound bite from a police detective. The video showed nighttime video of police at the crime scene. The reporter said the following: "The latest victim told police that her attacker spoke both English and Spanish and warned that he had a knife and would kill her if she resisted." The reporter closed with what was described as a vague description of the suspect.

KMBC–TV, Kansas City, MO.   Following Monday Night Football on this ABC affiliate, viewers saw videotape of the aftermath of an early morning fatal accident involving police. A sound bite from a daughter of one of the victims is heard: "There wasn't a siren. I'll take that one to court. No apology, no nothing. I mean, you need to tell me something if you killed my daddy." An anchor read the following: "Shock and anger for two Kansas City families tonight, and they want answers." A reporter live in the newsroom was following the investigation of the deaths of two people in a car hit by the police car. A witness said the police cruiser entered the intersection without lights and siren, as officers rushed to help other officers on a stolen car chase.

KTVN–TV, Reno, NV.   Following a lead story about wildfires, the Reno, NV, CBS affiliate told viewers the following: "The trial of three men accused of killing a Sparks paraplegic woman began today." The station rolled file courtroom footage and video of the crime scene. As they showed a still photo of the victim, the anchor said the victim "… was reportedly shot with the type of bullet designed to give a slow, painful death." The voice-over closed with the anchor on camera and an over-the-shoulder graphic of the scales of justice.

WSVN-TV, Miami, FL.   In Miami, FL, the reputation of sensationalized crime coverage for WSVN held for this sample week. The station opened Monday with the following: "Two girls attacked and raped at home called 911." With video of an audiocassette, the station played a police tape. The station continued its bump: "Tonight … the desperate call for help … after being tied up and terrorized." The station used the over-the-shoulder graphic of police lights as the anchor read, "This was a terrifying ordeal for them…. An attacker tying them up and raping them … and then as he turns to leave, he encourages them to call 911." Viewers were told that the victims were 11 and 12 years old. Later in the week, emphasis on crime was replaced by coverage of Hurricane Irene.

Tuesday, October 12, 1999

On Tuesday, three of the four networks (ABC, CNN, and NBC) led with a military coup in Pakistan and the nuclear concerns raised. This story was second on CBS. The CBS News led with the release of the Columbine High School surveillance videotapes. ABC followed up with more on the nuclear test ban

WSVN, Fox 7, Miami, Hurricane Irene.

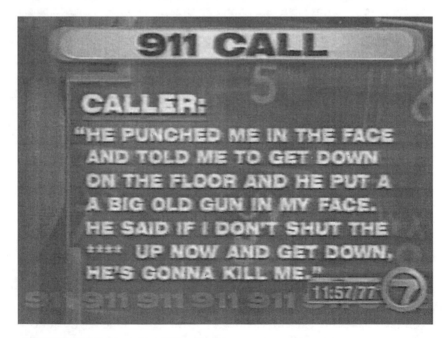

WSVN, Fox7, Miami, graphic of 911 transcript.

treaty under consideration by the Senate that week. Other stories receiving prominent national play on this day included the following: the death of basketball great Wilt Chamberlain, the United Nations report that global population had reached six billion, and a preview of the expected return of the JonBenet Ramsey Grand Jury in Boulder, CO. These latter three stories received significant attention from several of the local stations, although some markets led with uniquely local crime stories.

KXJB–TV, Fargo, ND.   On Tuesday night, the Fargo station led with the inadvertent release of the Columbine High video: "The tragedy at Columbine High School in Colorado is being relived through a chilling piece of videotape." The station first showed a brief clip of the cafeteria video, and then an anchor introduced the story about the surveillance camera footage. There was an over-the-shoulder graphic showing an aerial view of the high school and the words "INSIDE COLUMBINE." The CBS network report showed what appeared to be the beginning moments of the school shooting 6 months before. KXJB showed the video of students hiding under tables and then dashing away after shots appeared to be fired. It was video Denver, CO, stations declined to show.

KSTP–TV, Minneapolis, MN.   In Minneapolis, MN, the ABC affiliate reported on the charges filed against a man who allegedly molested two boys in a day care center. The station showed the outside of the building, a mug shot, and a map of the suburban Minneapolis area, as an anchor explained that the man was charged with "fondling" boys ages 4 and 5. A reporter was live in the studio as the station told viewers about the new charges against the 35-year-old man. Two months earlier, he had been charged with touching a 9-year-old family member. The reporter package showed children on the playground from a distance, slightly out of focus. A parent of a girl who attended the center and a day care spokesperson were interviewed.

KXAS–TV, Dallas–Ft. Worth, TX.   The NBC affiliate in Dallas–Ft. Worth, TX, joined stations in Los Angeles and Chicago in leading with the death of former basketball star Wilt Chamberlain on Tuesday night of the research period. The station led the second segment with a pair of breaking news stories. The first, from near San Antonio, TX, was a story about the wounding of at least two and as many as five police officers during a "manhunt" for a prison escapee. The male anchor read the story with an over-the-shoulder "BREAKING NEWS" graphic. The second story was read by the female anchor, and was about "… a man called Dallas' worst sexual offender ever." The man's photo and last name were featured in an over-the-shoulder graphic. A warrant had been issued for his arrest after he violated parole. The man had served 8 years of a 16-year prison sentence for molesting more than 40 boys at a Dallas YMCA, and had been at a halfway house for about 2 weeks. The station noted that police had not said how the man violated his parole.

WKYT–TV, Lexington, KY.   The lead bump and second story in the late evening news was a voice-over. It began with the anchor reading and an over-the-shoulder graphic of a gun barrel and two bullet holes labeled "LEXINGTON SHOOTING." The video showed yellow crime scene tape, police investigators, and flashing lights. Police were shown looking inside the car. The anchor said police were investigating a shooting of a man in the passenger seat of a car on the city's north side: "Police say he was hit by two or three bullets, but was conscious when taken to U.K. Hospital. Police are looking for three suspects."

KPTM–TV, Omaha, NE.   The Fox affiliate in Omaha, NE, teased their late evening newscast with the following: "Fire investigators are seeing more arson in the metro. We'll tell you how they're trying to snuff the problem." In the lead story, apartment house fire file footage was shown as an anchor read the following: "Seven fires in less than 7 days.... Investigators are trying to find those responsible for arson." An anchor read an introduction to the package with an over-the shoulder graphic of a lit match stick with the word "Arson." The reporter interviewed a woman and showed her small child, explaining that she had been awakened when fire broke out the previous night. A fire department spokesperson said the arson fires were not known to be related. The station showed the city's arson hotline telephone number.

Wednesday, October 13,1999

The NBC Nightly News was preempted by a baseball playoff game. ABC and CBS led with the admission from the Philip Morris tobacco company that smoking causes cancer, a story not covered by CNN in that newscast. CNN led with the continuing crisis in Pakistan, and the other two networks also covered this story. CBS and CNN mentioned imminent release of the Grand Jury report in the JonBenet Ramsey murder investigation, but ABC did not. The local stations focused on the Ramsey story as new information for their late newscast. At the same time, some stations had localized crime coverage.

KXJB–TV, Fargo, ND.   The CBS affiliate in Fargo, ND, led with the escape of a convicted child molester and killer. The opening graphic showed the photo and name of Kyle Bell, and the word "ESCAPED" in a red box. The story was characterized as "Breaking news out of New Mexico tonight." The convicted murderer was being transported from North Dakota to a prison in Oregon via New Mexico. He escaped at a truck stop while being moved by a private company that "ships prisoners across the country." The station took a live feed from the CBS affiliate KRQE, Albuquerque, NM. The reporter said there was an active search for the man. The Fargo station closed the story with local reaction from the county prosecutor who said he was frustrated by the escape.

KOAT, Santa Fe, ABC 7, action news zero tolerance on speeding.

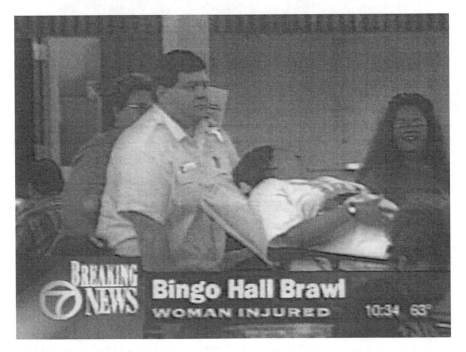

Koat, Santa Fe, ABC 7, bingo hall brawl.

KOAT–TV, Santa Fe, NM.   The 10 o'clock news also led with the "man-hunt" for "convicted child killer" Kyle Bell. The station opened with file footage courthouse video of the escapee. Bell was described as a "dangerous murderer" being transported from North Dakota when he used a key to get loose in Santa Rosa, NM. The station showed Christmas Eve home video of the victim from before her death. The anchor read that the man was serving a life sentence for "killing an 11-year-old girl in Fargo, North Dakota, and dumping her body into a river." During the week, the station also did a live shot on "zero tolerance" speed limits, and a breaking news story on a "bingo hall brawl."

KDLH–TV, Duluth, MN.   The lead story for the CBS affiliate in Duluth, MN, was about how a 7-year-old Wisconsin boy was "reunited" with his mother. He had been taken from a babysitter's house by his father who violated a custody order. The story was a voice-over using an exterior shot of the babysitter's house and a series of still photos of the boy and the man. This was the only local crime story reported in Duluth the entire week.

KIVI–TV, Boise, ID.   This station featured no local crime stories on this evening. The station did provide national coverage of the JonBenet Ramsey Grand Jury in Denver, CO. For the entire research week, this was the only station in the sample to have no local crime news. Further study revealed that there is crime news reported in the market, but none made it on the air for this station during the week.

Thursday, October 14, 1999

Three of the four networks (ABC, CBS, and NBC) led with the Senate rejection of the nuclear arms control treaty. That story was second on CNN. They led with the continuing crisis in Pakistan. ABC, CBS, and NBC followed up with 2nd-day coverage of the JonBenet Ramsey Grand Jury. Another story that received airtime was the progress of Hurricane Irene. None of these stories received much local station coverage by the time of the late evening newscast.

KCNC–TV, Denver, CO.   The CBS affiliate in Denver, CO, followed 3 days of coverage of the JonBenet Ramsey Grand Jury and Matthew Shepard murder trial in neighboring Laramie, WY, with a spot news story on Thursday night. A man claiming to have a bomb strapped to his body led to a police stand-off and traffic snarl in downtown Denver over the lunch-hour. The 10 p.m. newscast showed a city cam live shot of the street "back to normal" and "nothing like the nightmare" earlier in the day. A live shot from the scene introduced the piece. The dramatic video showed the man clinging to the Pioneer Monument. Three of the city's busiest streets had been closed for 3 hours. The reporter claimed "News 4 has chosen not to identify" the man; however, as those words were spoken, the video showed his leaflet with his name clearly visible. The station labeled as "creative" and "drastic" the way police diffused the situation: law enforcement officers posed as a TV news crew and "interviewed" the man. He then turned over his backpack and surrendered. Police later determined he had road flares rather than dynamite.

WLS–TV, Chicago, IL.   The ABC owned station in Chicago appeared to make a conscious decision to downplay local crime in its 10 p.m. newscast. Four out of 5 nights, this station led with national news, including Wilt Chamberlain's death and the JonBenet Ramsey Grand Jury decision not to indict. On Thursday evening, a night when the station led with a local story about a wheel coming off a jet airplane, the station did a brief voice-over in the second segment: "A deadly police chase on the southwest side." The 15-sec story began with a still photo of the woman who died. She had been spotted by police "driving erratically" and was chased until her car slammed into a utility pole. The only murder reported that week was on Friday night, a broadcast in which the station led with Hurricane Irene. The minute-long story, which ran fourth in the newscast, was about the first murder

KCNC, CBS 4, Denver, over-the shoulder graphic. Anchor updates child murder story.

in 6 years in a North Shore suburb and focused on domestic violence that apparently caused the crime. The station showed crime scene video and a sound bite with a family member.

Friday, October 15, 1999

All four major network newscasts led with an economic report concerning the largest 1-week drop in the Dow Jones stock index. ABC, CBS, and NBC all had Hurricane Irene's arrival in Florida as their second story, whereas CNN stayed with the Pakistan coup. A smattering of other stories included such topics as campaign finance reform, the award of a Nobel Peace Prize, and the airlift of an ill doctor from the Antarctic. These stories were not lead material for the local television stations.

WPDE–TV, Florence–Myrtle Beach, SC.   The ABC affiliate led with reaction to the state Supreme Court's decision to ban video poker machines. The second story was a voice-over "Update" on a volunteer firefighter freed from jail on arson charges involving two elementary schools. The station showed file footage of the fires and a mug shot. A jury was deadlocked on the charges. At the same time, forthcoming Hurricane Irene impacted coverage. One anchor and the station meteorologist were stationed at a coastal live shot.

WKYT–TV, Lexington, KY.   The CBS affiliate in Lexington, KY, reported the 40-year sentence of a man convicted of setting his girlfriend on fire and killing her. The story began with the anchor reading and an over-the-shoulder graphic of a gavel. The judge, the man, and his attorney were shown in the courtroom. The convicted killer claimed it was an accident and "made a plea for a lesser sentence." Viewers were told that the judge followed the jury's recommended sentence, and they saw the man's attorney interviewed outside the courtroom saying they would appeal. The story closed with the anchor reading that the man would serve 11 more years before being eligible for parole.

WBNS–TV, Columbus, OH.   The CBS affiliate led with the following: "A Columbus woman has a tale of terror to tell us about tonight." The station showed a graphic that read the following: "Carjacking Case. Picked Up Hitch-Hiker. Pulled a Gun. Woman Found." A hitchhiking hand, a hand with a gun, and a school building were shown. Viewers were told that the woman victim was found 2 days after the kidnapping "alive but scared." The live shot featured a reporter at the rear of a car, showing how the woman escaped from a car trunk. She pushed out the seat and struggled to the front ("even though her feet were duct taped") and honked the horn for help. A reporter honked a car horn as he told about how the woman rolled out into the street for help. The station interviewed coworkers at a Bob Evans restaurant. The story ended with a verbal description of the suspect in the case.

IMPLICATIONS OF LOCAL TV NEWS CONTENT

The content analysis established that crime coverage continues to be a mainstay of local television news broadcasts. Newscast producers acknowledge that live reports and dramatic video are important, and this may help explain why crime is an integral part of local television news. The decisions that local producers make appear to devalue issue-oriented national and international stories of the day. National news stories that do get heavy play on the late evening local news are easy-to-tell items, sensational events or natural disasters, dramatic crimes, coverage of well-known people, unusual video, and interesting features. A late breaking story also may have special value because of its timeliness.

Viewers who get their news only from a late evening local broadcast would not be likely to learn details about most national and international affairs. For example, during the week under study, hardly a mention was made on the local stations of the nuclear test ban treaty vote—a story that received lead coverage on the networks. Local news people might say that their first and most important job is to cover local news. However, at that hour of the evening, viewers have no over-the-air option for coverage of national and international news.

As stated earlier, 39% of the public has said they turned to local TV news for national and international stories, second only to cable news (Roper Center, 1999a), but only 16% say local TV news is doing the best job of covering the news, behind cable and network TV (Roper Center, 1999c). Perhaps there is a portion of the population who would prefer that local television news producers give more time to issue-oriented national and international stories.

At the same time, market size appears to influence news judgment. A 1994 study of late evening newscasts in 25 markets found that the large market stations were more likely to send reporters into the field to cover sensational stories (crime and courts, accidents and disasters, war and defense, human interest, and popular amusements), whereas the small market stations were inclined to rely on network feeds of sensational, human interest news from around the country (Carroll & Tuggle, 1997):

> ... We found that small-market stations imported greater proportions of sensational news than those in larger markets. Moreover, the proportion of sensational news they imported was greater than the proportion they originated locally. It was as if a lack of local sensationalistic news compelled decision makers to import enough to give their viewers a sufficient dose. (p. 129)

Crime news, then, may be considered within a larger category of market-driven news (McManus, 1994). However, it can be argued that crime news is most important because of dramatic portrayal, the nature of newsroom deci-

sions about coverage, and the potential influence on viewers. Crime may be de-
picted as an everyday happening close to home.

CHAPTER SUMMARY

Crime news coverage continues to play an important role in local television
newscasts. Business pressures and the competition for audience ratings drive
the decision to emphasize local crime stories. News managers were split on the
importance of crime news, but more agreed than disagreed that they often lead
with crime stories. The news directors and assignment editors agreed that spot
news and dramatic video were the key components in crime coverage, but they
disagreed that graphic video should be shown. A 1999 content analysis of local
television newscasts reflected a continued reliance on crime news coverage
and little attention to national and international issues.

DISCUSSION QUESTIONS

1. Explain the roles of assignment editor and producer in a local television
    newsroom. Do stations in your market appear to fit the national model?
2. How do your local stations cover crime? From your observations, do all of
    the stations follow the same approach?
3. Why do you think news managers agree with the use of dramatic video in
    crime coverage? Why do you think they shy away from graphic video?
    Have you seen crime news video that you thought went too far?
4. Besides graphic video, how else do local television reporters and produc-
    ers dramatize crime coverage? What role do photographers play in the
    process?
5. How do competitive pressures for audience ratings influence the thinking
    of local television newsroom employees? How does their thinking impact
    on what we see?

4

Legal Aspects of Crime
News Coverage

There is "no constitutional right of access to the scenes of crime or disaster when the general public is excluded."

—(Branzburg v. Hayes, 1972)

This chapter focuses on normative legal theories that apply to crime coverage on local TV news. The emphasis is on case law and its practical application. As Hermanson (2000) observed: "Journalists report on legal issues as interpreted by officials in court and non-court settings, and they must be able to determine goals of laws and how they should be applied to an orderly society" (p. 1). Nevertheless, it is also true that local television news people sometimes face obstacles in obtaining information about crimes or access to crime scenes.

CRIMINAL LAW AND CIVIL LAW

Local television news reporters "analyze and write stories on arrests, court decisions.... They must cover crime; report accurately on local, state and federal trials" (Hermanson, 2000, p. 1). Therefore, the emphasis on crime reporting in local television news coverage means that legal issues are very important in newsrooms. Further, media "construct accounts of trials which set up expectations in the minds of the public" (Howitt, 1998, p. 171). Criminal law involves the state's prosecution of individuals for violations of statutes that prohibit such acts as murder, armed robbery, assault, rape, or arson:

> The goal of criminal law is to promote an orderly society where people can feel secure. The government punishes violators to promote the common good, not to provide retribution for victims. In criminal cases, the state punishes viola-

tors—usually with fines or jail sentences.... Judges have some latitude in punishment, but usually the options are stated in statutes. (Hermanson, 2000, p. 11)

The burden in such cases is on a prosecutor to prove that the defendant is guilty beyond a reasonable doubt of specific charges. Often, where guilt is obvious, prosecutors and defense attorneys negotiate a plea bargain—an admission of guilt in exchange for reduction of charges and a lighter prison sentence. Criminal law, the subject of most crime coverage, is distinguished from civil law where one person sues another for monetary damages because of an injury: "Civil law usually involves a dispute between two private parties, with the government merely providing a neutral forum for resolving the dispute by balancing rights" (Hermanson, 2000, p. 10). For example, consider the case of an unlicensed truck driver who, following an evening at a tavern, crashes his semi rig into a teenager's sports car in a head-on collision. Under criminal law, if the truck driver survives, he will be charged with a series of violations—driving under the influence, driving without a proper license, vehicular homicide. Under civil law, the teen's family may sue directly the driver, his employer, and even the truck manufacturer for millions of dollars in damages.

There are state and federal trial courts where criminal and civil charges may be heard by a jury or judge. These courts determine the facts in a particular case. For example, civil lawsuits following a school shooting may determine if there was negligence on the part of an adult that led to a youth obtaining a handgun. All decisions of trial courts may be appealed for legal but not factual reasons. The 50 states each have their own court systems, and these run in addition to our federal courts. The coverage of crime news in the United States is guided by free speech philosophy that encourages legal processes to be conducted in public view.

THE FIRST AMENDMENT AND FREE EXPRESSION

As early as 1644, English philosopher John Milton articulated what became known later as "the marketplace of ideas" view that truths and falsehoods should compete for acceptance. Freedom of the press was seen as an important way for the public to learn (Sunstein, 1993) about the actions of their government (Levy, 1985). In the United States, the Constitution followed an early use of prior restraint doctrine—the government had no right to censor speech, but speakers may be held accountable for the consequences of their communication (*Near v. Minnesota*, 1931). Speech that is political in nature is assumed to have the strongest protection because it is vital to the functioning of democratic participation (Smolla, 1992). In contrast, broadcasting, coverage of crime and the courts, and potentially libelous comments have somewhat less protection. In the 1970s, Nebraska reporters attempting to cover arraignment of a suspect in a killing spree were ordered to not report testimony or evidence, but the Supreme Court found the gag order unconsti-

In October 1975 Erwin Simants raped and murdered a 10-year-old girl, and then killed five family members. At his arraignment, a county judge issued a broad gag order prohibiting publication of any information from the pretrial proceedings. The order ran counter to state law that required open courtrooms. Ultimately, the Supreme Court ruled in favor of the press. Chief Justice Burger wrote for a unanimous court:

> ... If it can be said that a threat of criminal or civil sanctions after publication "chills" speech, prior restrain "freezes" it at least for the time.

> The damage can be particularly great when the prior restraint falls upon the communication of news and commentary on current events. Truthful reports of public judicial proceedings have been afforded special protection against subsequent punishment.... It is not asking too much to suggest that those who exercise First Amendment rights in newspapers or broadcasting enterprises direct some effort to protect the rights of an accused to a fair trial by unbiased jurors.... (Nebraska Press v. Stuart, 1976, p. 559)

> ... We reaffirm that the guarantees of freedom of expression are not an absolute prohibition under all circumstances, but the barriers to prior restraint remain high and the presumption against its use continues intact. (p. 570)

Source: Nebraska Press Assn. v. Stuart, 427 U.S. 539 (1976).

BOX 4.1   *Nebraska Press Assn. v. Stuart* (1976).

tutional because a defendant's Sixth Amendment right to a fair trial must be balanced against news media First Amendment rights to report news (*Nebraska Press Assn. v. Stuart*, 1976).

Libel, Slander, and Defamation

Outside the context of a criminal case, a station itself may allege that an individual has violated the law. This is sometimes done by local television news investigative "I-Team" units and raises potential legal issues. The reporting of allegations in advance of formal charges by authorities may prompt a libel suit.

An individual claiming to be defamed by a local television news reporter could file a civil lawsuit against the reporter and his or her employer. The claim would be that the story unfairly places the person in a bad light with the public. Libel law relies on the fact that news coverage may harm someone's reputation, and this may lead to a loss of income or a job, loss of relationships with others, or loss of a positive reputation. In court, the individual's attorney would need to prove that the defamation was false information that identified the individual. If the person were not a public figure or official, then a showing that the newsroom acted negligently would be sufficient. If the person were a public figure or official, the "actual malice" standard is applied. It requires that it be proven that the reporters and editors knew the story was false or recklessly disregarded evidence (*New York Times v. Sullivan*, 1964).

The libel law standards make it extremely difficult for a plaintiff, particularly one who has a public life, to sustain a libel suit against a local television station. In such a case, lawyers for a television station may use truth of the allegations as the ultimate defense. Even where reporting harms reputation, reporting the truth, if it can be proven factual, is protected under the Constitution and the First Amendment. Further, expressions of opinions by local television news reporters have also been found to be protected by some judges (*KTRK v. Turner*, 1998).

Because the *New York Times v. Sullivan* (1964) case placed the burden of proving a story to be false on a plaintiff, and because media defendants have become adept at fighting lawsuits, lawyers have begun to move away from libel suits against television stations and toward the use of laws designed to restrict investigative news gathering techniques, such as hidden-camera investigations (*Food Lion v. ABC*, 1997). In most crime coverage, the release of public information through police and attorneys insulates local television newsrooms from the threat of libel or other civil suits.

Invasion of Privacy

Likewise, the concept of invasion of privacy has been the subject of cases against television stations in recent decades. The so-called tort law involves legal responsibilities of individuals. Invasion of privacy has been defined as reporting embarrassing private facts, intrusion into one's solitude, trespassing on private property, placing someone in a false light, or using one's name or likeness for commercial gain without permission (Splichal, 2000).

In Portland, OR, KATU–TV was sued by an automobile accident victim after the station shot video and used it for a news promo on another story. The state's Supreme Court held that the station's newsworthiness defense insulated it from a lawsuit claiming privacy had been violated and the victim's image had been appropriated for commercial use without consent. Under Oregon law, the station was allowed to lawfully gather the video, although airing of the video might cause hurt feelings (*Anderson v. Fisher Broadcasting*, 12 Med.L.Rptr. 1604, Ore. 1986).

Local television news reporters and photographers may open their stations to liability if they trespass on private property, or violate other laws, to obtain a story. In most crime reporting, invasion of privacy is not at issue because there is a public crime scene. Once evidence has been collected, the action moves to the public courts and records. Generally, local television newsrooms have wide access to gather video.

In Seattle, WA, KING–TV was sued for defamation and invasion of privacy after it reported on a pharmacist charged with Medicaid fraud. The station reported the following in December 1976: "A West Seattle pharmacist has been charged with defrauding the state of $200,000 for false drug prescriptions...." As part of the story, the station aired video of the pharmacist talking on the telephone inside the business. The photographer was standing outside the pharmacy and shot video through a glass window. The pharmacist claimed that the video aired was "an unreasonable intrusion into his seclusion and physical solitude" (Mark v. King Broadcasting, 1980, p. 518). The court, however, determined that such an invasion could only be actionable if "highly offensive and objectionable to the ordinary person":

> The invasion or intrusion must be of something which the general public would not be free to view. Here, it is not contended that the film recorded anything other than that which any passerby would have seen passing the building, nor was the plaintiff portrayed in an unreasonable manner. The filming was accomplished without ruse or subterfuge. There is no reason to believe that a person of ordinary sensibilities would be offended by the film alone. (Mark v. King Broadcasting, 1980, p. 519)

The court ruled in favor of the TV station, in part, because the pharmacist was "entangled in this web of news and public interest" (p. 52). The libel aspect of the lawsuit also could not be sustained because in 1976 KING–TV had truthfully reported the public record, and it had not in any way embellished the story. In fact, during the summer of 1977 the pharmacist was convicted on 5 counts of forgery and grand larceny. Courts more generally have ruled that crimes, prosecutions, and court proceedings "... are without question events of legitimate concern to the public and consequently fall within the responsibility of the press to report the operations of government" (p. 516).

Source: Mark v. King Broadcasting Co., Wash. App., 618 P.2d 512 (1980)

BOX 4.2   Mark v. King Broadcasting (1980).

Access at Crime Scenes

The courts have ruled that local television news reporters and photographers have no special right of access to crime scenes (Branzburg v. Hayes, 1972), but this does not prevent enterprising employees from obtaining all the information available to any member of the general public. In most states, reporters may be excluded from or moved back away from crime or disaster scenes, so officials may do their work. In general, media rights to report must be balanced against other concerns. The traditions of local communities with respect to the rules governing local media seem most important in judging behavior at the scene of breaking news events.

Local TV news reporters have a strong interest in obtaining video and sound bites from crime scenes. Usually, such stories demand live shots on the late evening news. The access to crime scenes and official spokespersons make the stories relatively easy to produce. Further, the First Amendment insulation from subsequent punishment for the broadcast of these stories means that they are legally safe. Nevertheless, there may be some concern by newsroom employees about how far they can go.

Access to Public Records and Freedom of Information

Federal and state open records laws provide local television newsrooms with a right of access to information that is part of the public record. For example, although Grand Jury proceedings investigating a crime are not public, an official indictment of someone for a crime would become part of the public record. Similarly, police investigative files are not public, but reporters do have access to crime reports and arrest reports. When a case goes to trial, much information that previously was not public is entered into the public record. Public records are a key source of information for crime reporters because accurate reporting of it is protected under libel law defenses. Often, when officials do not make themselves available for comment during investigation of a crime, reporters may rely on public records. For example, if prosecutors obtain a search warrant from a local judge, the existence of a warrant as a public record may be a clue for investigative news reporters.

In Illinois, media have run into trouble with a uniform media arrest report law. The rules specify what information must be released. Although reporters are supposed to have access to the name, age, address, and photograph of someone arrested, authorities have up to 72 hr to comply. The Illinois Press Association in March 2000 complained of news "blackouts" caused by county prosecuting state's attorneys refusing to release information such as criminal histories. The state Supreme Court directed the attorneys to limit their interaction with news media (Illinois Press Association, 2000).

News Routines and the Police Beat

Most initial crime coverage occurs because news assignment editors monitor police radios, telephone tips from viewers, competing television coverage, other media such as radio news, and official tips. The first stage of such coverage involves local television newsrooms rushing personnel to the scene to try to obtain accurate information (Graber, 1997). Those newsrooms that assign a police beat reporter may do daily checks of police records, detectives offices, and other routine locations searching for new stories to cover or follow up information on older news. Over time, some news reporters establish relation-ships with police sources, and these may lead authorities to provide certain reporters with special access to information. In general, however, the public sometimes lacks support for full First Amendment press freedoms (McLeod, Sitrovic, Voakes, Guo, & Huang, 1998).

Coverage of the Courts

Local television news coverage of the courts involves stations deciding which few crime cases are important enough to be considered for continuing cover-age. This involves news values, and it also involves relationships reporters have with prosecutors, defense attorneys, judges, and other courthouse personnel (Lipschultz, 1991). Local television stations generally do not have enough re-porters for beat coverage of the courts, and they tend to rely on day-to-day de-cisions. Sources become important in making decisions about whether anything newsworthy will occur on a particular day of a trial that could take months to complete.

Television news is a visual medium, and some jurisdictions do not allow tele-vision cameras inside the courtroom. Others limit access to a single pool cam-era. Therefore, we often see news photographers outside of courtrooms to get usable shots of the accused and victims. In the era of modern public relations, trial lawyers sometimes hold news conferences to make their cases to the public.

Courthouse coverage is important to local television news people because the trial is the place where lurid details of a criminal case first become available. Lawyers may argue about, for example, the admission into evidence of some facts outside the presence of the jury. Access to the courtroom proceedings means that the public is privy to information through the news media that may be interesting but not very relevant to the outcome of a case. This is because lawyers are limited by judicial rules about what information may be used in a criminal case. Failure of a judge to rule correctly could lead to a conviction be-ing overturned on appeal.

Cameras and the Courthouse

Before television, there was concern about the use of still photography inside the courtroom because the noisy cameras and flashbulbs were disruptive (Bittner, 1994). In the 1960s, the case of fraudulent Texas businessman Billie Sol Estes brought to the forefront the issue of television cameras in the court-room. At first, the trial judge allowed TV coverage of portions of the trial. In re-versing Estes's conviction, the United States Supreme Court identified four areas in which TV could interfere with the defendant's right to a fair trial: (a) TV may impact a jury, (b) TV may influence testimony, (c) the supervision of TV coverage may distract the trial judge, and (d) TV may harass the defendant

(*Estes v. State of Texas*, 381 U.S. 532, 1965). Changes in technology led to television equipment that is quieter, smaller, and less disruptive. Additionally, most judges limit access to a single "pool" TV camera from a location pointing away from the jury box. The video feed from the camera is made available to all news outlets.

Although most state courts allow TV camera and microphone access to the courtroom, most federal courtrooms do not. It is still common to see television newsrooms use artist sketches of courtroom proceedings in situations where cameras are barred.

Outside the courtroom or courthouse, reporters and photographers routinely gather in hopes of obtaining video and sound bites from lawyers, defendants, victims and their family members, and even jurors. Judicial rules may limit what participants may say. Local TV newsrooms are often contacted by law enforcement personnel when a defendant will be taken from the jail to the courthouse, so that stations can get video. Some courtrooms now use video feeds from the jail to avoid transporting prisoners. These feeds are usually available to local media.

Local Television News and the Law

The importance of local news media participation, as surrogate for the public, in the search for justice, has come to be understood in American law (*Richmond Newspapers v. Virginia*, 1980). The Supreme Court has based a right of open pretrial and trial proceedings on the need for defendants to be protected against lawyers and judges that might participate in an unfair process (*Press Enterprise v. Riverside County Superior Court*, 1986). None of this prohibits a judge from closing proceeding for good reasons. For example, juvenile courts typically are closed to coverage by all local news media, including television stations. Of course, any ruling by a judge is open to appeal by news organizations or others.

Local television newsrooms continue to be prohibited from bringing their cameras, what the Radio Television News Directors Association has termed "tools of their trade," into most federal courtrooms and some state courts. Also, broadcasting generally has less protection against broader control by government regulators such as the Federal Communication Commission (*Red Lion Broadcasting Co. v. FCC*, 1969). Nevertheless, overall local television newsrooms have broad First Amendment protections in the United States to cover those crime stories that meet journalistic news values. The First Amendment prohibition against government restrictions on the press, as Hopkins (2000) observed, "establish the essence of democracy" (p. v). In this sense, although we sometimes take issue with the decisions made by local television newsrooms, their right to challenge the social order is crucial to a legal structure that values freedom and social responsibility over rigid government control. There are no easy answers: "The pervasive nature of electronic media continues to strain the boundaries between a defendant's right to a fair trial and the right to gather news" (Creech, 2000, p. 303). Therefore, ethical concerns become of primary importance in evaluating the decisions made by local television newsroom employees. As one news director told the Radio and Television News Directors Foundation:

> With crews armed with hand-held cameras, able to return video from virtually anywhere, the problem of editorial oversight becomes even more difficult to address. With images coming at a thinly staffed newsroom … judgments that are fair and accurate will have to be made on the spot. (1995, pp. 11–12)

Although communication law in the United States does not limit local television news coverage of crime stories, live TV news technology has decreased the time during which newsroom personnel may consider the ethics of their decisions.

CHAPTER SUMMARY

Local television newsrooms cover crime in America under a legal system that provides reporters, photographers, producers, assignment editors, and news directors wide latitude to meet the perceived needs and wants of audience members. Particularly when they cover breaking news events, official proceedings such as trials, and obtain documentary information from the public record, they are protected to report truthful facts, so long as they abide by reasonable access limitations.

DISCUSSION QUESTIONS

1. Does modern local news coverage of crime promote an orderly society? Why or why not?
2. How might civil laws affect a local station's crime coverage? Are they more or less important than criminal laws?
3. Do you think libel laws have a "chilling effect" on decisions to cover certain crime stories?
4. If you were a videographer at the scene of a homicide, would you walk onto the property to get a good shot? Why or why not?
5. Do you agree with the reasoning that some television stations should be barred from bringing their camera inside a courtroom because they may be disruptive to the rights of a defendant to receive a fair trial? How do such rules measure up to our understanding of the meaning of the First Amendment?

5

Ethics

by Chris W. Allen
University of Nebraska at Omaha

"A journalist must care about doing the right thing, must want to be ethical; such a sincere desire will lead the journalist to seek out moral wisdom as a guide to ethical decision making."

—John Merrill, ethics scholar (1997, p. 28)

Local television news did not invent coverage of crime. In fact, mass media have been covering violence for some 150 years. In this chapter the focus is on how media history has led to an interest in the issue of ethics.

A BRIEF HISTORY OF CRIME NEWS

At the turn of the 20th century, two of America's most notorious publishers, Joseph Pulitzer and William Randolph Hearst, were locked in a fierce circulation battle. Both announced their daily circulation on the front page, using a cartoon character called the Yellow Kid. Their respective newspapers, Pulitzer's *New York World* and Hearst's *New York Journal*, engaged in the foulest sensationalism, which came to be known as Yellow Journalism because of the Kid, in an effort to attract the most readers. In 1897, as America neared war with Spain over Cuba, Pulitzer's correspondent James Creelman, urging President McKinley to take some sort of action against Spain, wrote the following:

> No man's life, no man's property, is safe. American citizens are imprisoned or slain without cause. American property is destroyed on all sides.... Blood on the roadsides, blood in the fields, blood on the doorsteps, blood, blood, blood! (*World*, 1896, in Folkerts & Teeter, 1998, p. 269)

It was nothing new to the two papers. The Penny Press era introduced read-ers to scandal, murder, mayhem, riots, and corruption. Newsboys would stand on street corners hawking their papers by hollering out the lurid stories waiting to be read.

There were no codes of ethics in the 1800s. Readers expected sensational-ism, or at least exaggeration, in their newspapers. Journalists had not yet adopted a policy of fair and balanced reporting, and accuracy was on shaky ground.

Today, however, we expect more from our media—or should. Codes of ethics have been around for about 80 years. They have dealt with conflicts of interest, accuracy, fairness, influence, use of anonymous sources, and other problems com-mon to journalism. However, they have not dealt specifically with the question of violence.

Television has been consistently criticized for the violent content of its enter-tainment programs. Some studies have indicated that kids see 20,000 murders by the time they reach the age of 18. At one time in the 1980s the networks, in an effort to hold off threatened Congressional regulation, agreed to limit pro-grams that contained violence to time slots after the so-called "family hour," 8 to 9 p.m., Eastern Standard Time. For the most part, the four broadcast net-works still limit their violent programming to after 9 p.m.

Viewers, however, can see plenty of violence earlier in the day. Network eve-ning newscasts often contain the real violence of crime, war, and terrorism. Local broadcasts sometimes wallow in it. Although rarely is the act of killing shown, certainly the aftermath is a staple of nightly news programs across the United States. This becomes an ethical problem because of what violence in TV news-casts may do to the audience. *Washington Post* critic Tom Shales said violence on TV exaggerates people's fears about the world. It gives the impression that vio-lence is the norm (Jacobs, 1990).

ETHICS IN LOCAL TV NEWS TODAY

Examples abound of ethically questionable uses of violence in local newscasts, especially because TV stations make live coverage routine. One of the most vivid examples was the live scene of a bloodied Columbine High School stu-dent escaping from a window into the arms of heavily armored police.

When Los Angeles TV stations covered a man blocking traffic on a freeway, it was a chance to utilize high technology—live cameras and helicopters—to show people the news. Then the man set fire to his truck, pulled out a shotgun, and killed himself. Most stations did not react in time to cut the picture, and al-most everyone watching the incident on TV that day saw the suicide. Some sta-tions had broken into children's programming to show it (Chua-Eoan, 1998). Derwin Johnson, a former TV producer and now a professor at the Columbia University Graduate School of Journalism, says the decision to go live was a mis-

KUSA, Denver has coverage carried by CNN.

The shooting spree in April 1999 at Columbine High School in Colorado illustrates the tension between ethical decision making and the airing of live video in the midst of a crisis. When masked gunmen opened fire inside the school, Denver, CO, stations found themselves drawn into the middle of a breaking crime story.

A reporter for KMGH–TV acknowledged the possibility that hostages and the gunmen inside the school building could be watching events unfold on TV. "We are assuming they are able to watch all the coverage."

At first, local stations used graphics and telephone interviews. Eventually, live trucks provided video from the scene and interviews with students who had run out of the building. KUSA interviewed a student who told what it was like inside: "We hear some guy go 'holy crap, there's a guy with a gun.' So everybody starts freaking out.... My teacher just doesn't know what to do 'cause she's so freaked." Then, there was this exchange between anchors and a student:

Student: Is this live? Is this on?

Anchor: Yeah, are some of them still in there?

Student: Yeah, I think so. My sister was shot.

Anchor: Your sister. Is she going to the hospital? Is she outside with you right now, or is she still in the school?

Student: She went with the paramedics.

Anchor: Oh, that's good. Okay.

KCNC showed video of injured students being taken to an ambulance, and they did dramatic telephone interviews with upset students who had escaped. KUSA quickly brought their "Sky 9" helicopter to the scene to show wide shots of the school.

At one point, a student trapped in the school used a cell phone to call KUSA. He described the scene while hiding under a desk inside a classroom. The student started to say where he was before an anchor stopped him and urged him to call 911. The student found the 911 line jammed, and placed another call to the station, which connected him with the emergency line.

Later in the coverage, as students pleaded for help and tried to escape, live video showed an injured victim. An anchor at KMGH–TV gasped, "Look at that!" as a blood-streaked youth dropped from a second-story window. Her coanchor expressed disbelief "that this could happen in our area."

At another point, KUSA urged trapped students to call the station with information for the police on the gunmen's whereabouts. Anchor Kim Christiansen said, "Any students that might be hiding at the school, call the station.... We will put you in touch with the police." But minutes later, Christiansen retracted those instructions, saying, "Do not call the station. Be quiet. Stay where you are."

Throughout the day, televised images showed a shocking scene—the stricken faces of students and parents, the cluster of paramedics and SWAT teams, the chaotic aftermath. One girl told how she begged for her life while the gunmen waved a gun in her face, laughed, and asked her if she wanted to die. "He shot everybody around me," she said through sobs. A teenage boy told of seeing "a friend of mine's head blown off."

Playing a role that often falls to local TV when tragedy strikes, the Denver stations served as information clearinghouses. They gave parents telephone hotline numbers, and reminded them to "stay away from Columbine High School."

Sources: Don Aucoin, Denver stations provide lens and voice for tragedy. *Boston Globe,* April 21, 1999, p. A31; KUSA and KCNC via CNN, April 20, 1999.

BOX 5.1   Local TV News Coverage of Columbine High School Shooting.

take from the start. He calls it a "classic case of technology running the beast instead of a clear editorial process" (Chua-Eoan,1998, p. 30).

Violent news content is not exclusively the result of live coverage. In the 1980s, a TV station in Arkansas received a call about a bus hijacking. The hijackers, a man and a woman, wanted to talk to the reporter. The reporter and a photographer went to talk to them. The evening newscast aired a complete, edited, and scripted report. After talking with the pair, and showing part of the interview on air, the journalists retreated back behind police lines. The hijackers released the passengers from the bus, then, with camera rolling, shot themselves. The report showed the man and woman kneeling on the pavement, putting the guns to their heads, pulling the trigger, and crumpling to the ground. The journalists had plenty of time before the newscast to debate the ethics on several points:

1. *Airing the demands made by the hijackers*   Often TV broadcast outlets refuse to do that because it may encourage others to try the same tactic for publicity.
2. *Showing a double suicide*   When that tape was shown during a session on ethics at the 2000 Radio–Television News Directors Association (RTNDA) convention in Minneapolis, MN, most of the newsroom managers in the room cringed.

Ethical lapses often occur as local TV newsrooms struggle to make quick decisions on deadline. Hundreds of local TV stations produce thousands of hours of news a day. Most of the stations are competing against at least one other TV newsroom in the city or area, just as Pulitzer and Hearst battled each other 100 years ago. There are pressures on a TV journalist to get the story first. News directors, who always watch the competition, may confront a reporter who gets beat on a story, and the reporter may have some explaining to do (Smith, 1999). Such pressure to get the story and get it on the air first can push some reporters to meet a deadline rather than take the time to think completely through a story. Even news directors succumb. When one station broadcasts an incident live, others feel pressured to do the same.

The pressure to be first at all costs combined with the relative inexperience of some reporters is a dangerous mix. Brian Trauring, news director of WATE–TV in Knoxville, TN, and chair of the RTNDA Ethics Committee (which recently revamped the association's code of ethics), says many rookie reporters come into the job with poor news judgment and few decision-making skills. He says newsrooms have to do a better job of training the young reporters (Heyboer, 1999). However, Howard Rosenberg, TV columnist at the *Los Angeles Times*, disagreed. Rosenberg, who also teaches journalism ethics at the University of Southern California, says it is not a matter of training; the difference between right and wrong is obvious. The problem, he said, is not the reporters, but the competition for ratings (Heyboer, 1999).

Journalism students are getting at least some ethical training in school. In 1994 about 60% of journalism schools had an ethics course. Most of the programs that do not have a separate standing course teach ethics as a component of other courses. In a survey by Lambeth, Christians, and Cole (1994), nearly all instructors that were questioned said fostering moral reasoning skills was important. Ninety percent said surveying the current ethical practice of the pro-

PREAMBLE

Members of the Society of Professional Journalists believe that public enlightenment is the forerunner of justice and the foundation of democracy. The duty of the journalist is to further those ends by seeking truth and providing a fair and comprehensive account of events and issues. Conscientious journalists from all media and specialties strive to serve the public with thoroughness and honesty. Professional integrity is the cornerstone of a journalist's credibility. Members of the Society share a dedication to ethical behavior and adopt this code to declare the Society's principles and standards of practice.

SEEK TRUTH AND REPORT IT

Journalists should be honest, fair, and courageous in gathering, reporting, and interpreting information.

Journalists should

- Test the accuracy of information from all sources and exercise care to avoid inadvertent error. Deliberate distortion is never permissible.
- Diligently seek out subjects of news stories to give them the opportunity to respond to allegations of wrongdoing.
- Identify sources whenever feasible. The public is entitled to as much information as possible on sources' reliability.
- Always question sources' motives before promising anonymity. Clarify conditions attached to any promise made in exchange for information.
- Keep promises.
- Make certain that headlines, news teases, and promotional material, photos, video, audio, graphics, sound bites, and quotations do not misrepresent. They should not oversimplify or highlight incidents out of context.
- Never distort the content of news photos or video. Image enhancement for technical clarity is always permissible. Label montages and photo illustrations.
- Avoid misleading reenactments or staged news events. If reenactment is necessary to tell a story, label it.
- Avoid undercover or other surreptitious methods of gathering information except when traditional open methods will not yield information vital to the public. Use of such methods should be explained as part of the story.
- Never plagiarize.
- Tell the story of the diversity and magnitude of the human experience boldly, even when it is unpopular to do so.
- Examine their own cultural values and avoid imposing those values on others.

- Avoid stereotyping by race, gender, age, religion, ethnicity, geography, sexual orientation, disability, physical appearance, or social status.
- Support the open exchange of views, even views they find repugnant.
- Give voice to the voiceless; official and unofficial sources of information can be equally valid.
- Distinguish between advocacy and news reporting. Analysis and commentary should be labeled and not misrepresent fact or context.
- Distinguish news from advertising and shun hybrids that blur the lines between the two.
- Recognize a special obligation to ensure that the public's business is conducted in the open and that government records are open to inspection.

MINIMIZE HARM

Ethical journalists treat sources, subjects, and colleagues as human beings deserving of respect.

Journalists should

- Show compassion for those who may be affected adversely by news coverage. Use special sensitivity when dealing with children and inexperienced sources or subjects.
- Be sensitive when seeking or using interviews or photographs of those affected by tragedy or grief.
- Recognize that gathering and reporting information may cause harm or discomfort. Pursuit of the news is not a license for arrogance.
- Recognize that private people have a greater right to control information about themselves than do public officials and others who seek power, influence, or attention. Only an overriding public need can justify intrusion into anyone's privacy.
- Show good taste. Avoid pandering to lurid curiosity.
- Be cautious about identifying juvenile suspects or victims of sex crimes.
- Be judicious about naming criminal suspects before the formal filing of charges.
- Balance a criminal suspect's fair trial rights with the public's right to be informed.

ACT INDEPENDENTLY

Journalists should be free of obligation to any interest other than the public's right to know.

Journalists should

- Avoid conflicts of interest, real or perceived.

- Remain free of associations and activities that may compromise integrity or damage credibility.
- Refuse gifts, favors, fees, free travel, and special treatment, and shun secondary employment, political involvement, public office, and service in community organizations if they compromise journalistic integrity.
- Disclose unavoidable conflicts.
- Be vigilant and courageous about holding those with power accountable.
- Deny favored treatment to advertisers and special interests and resist their pressure to influence news coverage.
- Be wary of sources offering information for favors or money; avoid bidding for news.

BE ACCOUNTABLE

Journalists are accountable to their readers, listeners, viewers, and each other.

Journalists should

- Clarify and explain news coverage and invite dialogue with the public over journalistic conduct.
- Encourage the public to voice grievances against the news media.
- Admit mistakes and correct them promptly.
- Expose unethical practices of journalists and the news media.
- Abide by the same high standards to which they hold others.

Source: Sigma Delta Chi's first Code of Ethics was borrowed from the American Society of Newspaper Editors in 1926. In 1973, Sigma Delta Chi wrote its own code, which was revised in 1984 and 1987. The present version of the Society of Professional Journalists' Code of Ethics was adopted in September 1996.

BOX 5.2   Society of Professional Journalists Code of Ethics.

fession was important, and 92% said preparing students for professional work was important (Lambeth et al., 1994).

Ethics Codes

Codes of ethics are a voluntary way to encourage responsible journalism. The Society of Professional Journalists represents journalists from all fields, and has a code of ethics that has been revised over the years. However, although it calls for accuracy, fairness, and avoidance of outside influence, it does not address what kinds of stories to cover or ignore.

The RTNDA, wishing to foster the highest professional standards of electronic journalism, promote public understanding of and confidence in electronic journalism, and strengthen principles of journalistic freedom to gather and disseminate information, establishes this Code of Ethics and Professional Conduct.

PREAMBLE

Professional electronic journalists should operate as trustees of the public, seek the truth, report it fairly and with integrity and independence, and stand accountable for their actions.

PUBLIC TRUST

Professional electronic journalists should recognize that their first obligation is to the public.

Professional electronic journalists should

- Understand that any commitment other than service to the public undermines trust and credibility.
- Recognize that service in the public interest creates an obligation to reflect the diversity of the community and guard against oversimplification of issues or events.
- Provide a full range of information to enable the public to make enlightened decisions.
- Fight to ensure that the public's business is conducted in public.

TRUTH

Professional electronic journalists should pursue truth aggressively and present the news accurately, in context, and as completely as possible.

Professional electronic journalists should

- Continuously seek the truth.
- Resist distortions that obscure the importance of events.
- Clearly disclose the origin of information and label all material provided by outsiders.

Professional electronic journalists should not

- Report anything known to be false.
- Manipulate images or sounds in any way that is misleading.
- Plagiarize.
- Present images or sounds that are reenacted without informing the public.

FAIRNESS

Professional electronic journalists should present the news fairly and impartially, placing primary value on significance and relevance.

Professional electronic journalists should

- Treat all subjects of news coverage with respect and dignity, showing particular compassion to victims of crime or tragedy.
- Exercise special care when children are involved in a story and give children greater privacy protection than adults.
- Seek to understand the diversity of their community and inform the public without bias or stereotype.
- Present a diversity of expressions, opinions, and ideas in context.
- Present analytical reporting based on professional perspective, not personal bias.
- Respect the right to a fair trial.

INTEGRITY

Professional electronic journalists should present the news with integrity and decency, avoiding real or perceived conflicts of interest, and respect the dignity and intelligence of the audience as well as the subjects of news.

Professional electronic journalists should

- Identify sources whenever possible. Confidential sources should be used only when it is clearly in the public interest to gather or convey important information or when a person providing information might be harmed. Journalists should keep all commitments to protect a confidential source.
- Clearly label opinion and commentary.
- Guard against extended coverage of events or individuals that fails to significantly advance a story, place the event in context, or add to the public knowledge.
- Refrain from contacting participants in violent situations while the situation is in progress.
- Use technological tools with skill and thoughtfulness, avoiding techniques that skew facts, distort reality, or sensationalize events.
- Use surreptitious news gathering techniques, including hidden cameras or microphones, only if there is no other way to obtain stories of significant public importance and only if the technique is explained to the audience.
- Disseminate the private transmissions of others only with permission.

Professional electronic journalists should not

- Pay news sources who have a vested interest in a story.
- Accept gifts, favors, or compensation from those who might seek to influence coverage.
- Engage in activities that may compromise their integrity or independence.

INDEPENDENCE

Professional electronic journalists should defend the independence of all journalists from those seeking influence or control over news content.

Professional electronic journalists should

- Gather and report news without fear or favor, and vigorously resist undue influence from any outside forces, including advertisers, sources, story subjects, powerful individuals, and special interest groups.
- Resist those who would seek to buy or politically influence news content or who would seek to intimidate those who gather and disseminate the news.
- Determine news content solely through editorial judgment and not as the result of outside influence.
- Resist any self-interest or peer pressure that might erode journalistic duty and service to the public.
- Recognize that sponsorship of the news will not be used in any way to determine, restrict, or manipulate content.
- Refuse to allow the interests of ownership or management to influence news judgment and content inappropriately.
- Defend the rights of the free press for all journalists, recognizing that any professional or government licensing of journalists is a violation of that freedom.

ACCOUNTABILITY

Professional electronic journalists should recognize that they are accountable for their actions to the public, the profession, and themselves.

Professional electronic journalists should

- Actively encourage adherence to these standards by all journalists and their employers.
- Respond to public concerns. Investigate complaints and correct errors promptly and with as much prominence as the original report.
- Explain journalistic processes to the public, especially when practices spark questions or controversy.

- Recognize that professional electronic journalists are duty-bound to conduct themselves ethically.
- Refrain from ordering or encouraging courses of action which would force employees to commit an unethical act.
- Carefully listen to employees who raise ethical objections and create environments in which such objections and discussions are encouraged.
- Seek support for and provide opportunities to train employees in ethical decision making.

In meeting its responsibility to the profession of electronic journalism, RTNDA has created this code to identify important issues, to serve as a guide for its members, to facilitate self-scrutiny, and to shape future debate.

Source: Adopted at the RTNDA2000 International Conference in Minneapolis, MN, September 14, 2000.

BOX 5.3   Code of Ethics and Professional Conduct, Radio–Television News Directors Association.

The RTNDA spent 1999 and 2000 revising its code of ethics. As with the Society of Professional Journalists' code, and most codes, it does not address specific instances. Instead, it is general and open to broad interpretation. It can be adapted to different situations, including the coverage of violence.

In the pressure-cooker environment of many local television newsrooms, finishing the story on time is the sole goal. There is little time to contemplate ethical nuances. Christians, Fackler, Rotzoll, and McKee (2001) proposed using the Potter Box model of making decisions about ethics. The system involves a defined process to reach an ethical decision that begins with defining the problem in specific terms, identifying the relevant values to be considered, appealing to an ethical principle, then choosing where one's loyalties lie. Finally, a decision is made. There should be feedback among all the steps. But again the drawback is the time it takes to work through the box. It may take only 5 minutes, but on deadline the newsroom is not a welcoming environment, and while preparing for a live shot 5 minutes may be an impossible luxury.

Journalism educator John Merrill (1997) would rather see journalists develop an internal sense of ethics that does not rely on newsroom environment or culture. He also does not place much faith in codes. Merrill said journalists should act as individuals. Individual ethics means ethics are self-determined and voluntary. Although society must be considered in the decision, it is the individual, through self-reflection, who is ultimately responsible and no one else.

It is the intersection of individuals and codes where Merrill (1997) sees a potential for problems. Codes set a standard. Live up to the code, and you will be fine. There is no need to go beyond it. That is why Merrill warns against group-oriented ethics, including codes, that journalists tend to gravitate toward. The

TABLE 5.1

News Producers' Attitudes Toward Ethics in the Newsroom (Percentage)

	Strongly Disagree	Disagree	Neutral	Agree	Strongly Agree
It is important for a TV news-room to have a code of discussion of ethics.	1.1	4.6	11.5	39.1	34.7
Pressure for ratings points is causing an erosion of ethical standards in TV news.	1.1	9.2	9.2	55.2	25.3
A TV newsroom should adjust its ethics according to the story.	23.0	37.9	12.6	17.2	8.0

individual ethicist, in going beyond the professional or newsroom code, is seen as a poor team player, one who does not fit the world of corporate and competitive journalism. Working in a competitive situation, the individual feels the pressure to be right, to be graphic, to grab as much of the audience as possible. Newsroom managers and station managers may exert pressure to abandon individual ethics in favor of a corporate culture.

There appears to be a difference in decision making between young journalists with less than 6 years of experience and veterans with more than 6 years (Husselbee, 1997). The younger journalists tend to see themselves as strictly disseminators of news, and they tend to adhere strictly to the rules of reporting, including ethics codes. Those with more than 6 years of experience have become comfortable enough in the newsroom and in their own abilities to play a more interpretive role. These people are more able to take on the responsibility of making their own ethical and moral decisions.

Ethical Decision Making

Journalists may feel more confident in their ethical decision making as they gain experience, but they still feel pressure from "above." Allen, Lipschultz, and Hilt (1998) asked news producers their feelings about the ethical dynamics within the television newsroom. By far the majority of producers felt they want to be ethical but find it increasingly difficult in a corporate climate based on economics and ratings. They also think it is important to have a written code in the newsroom. However, it is also clear that they feel the competitive nature of the newsroom is eroding ethical standards. Perhaps most interesting is that producers feel ethics should be adjusted according to the story. They would fall among those who are not bound to rules, but see the rules as flexible and subject to interpretation.

Mass media decision making, such as the decision to show violence, is not always wrong. Pictures of bodies in a war zone add an element of depth and pathos needed to understand the horror. However, it comes in degrees. Americans seem to have no problem seeing the bodies of dead Palestinians in Israel, but they do not want to see bodies of tragic incidents in the United States. Large numbers of bodies are more acceptable than one body. A body, after the killing, is more acceptable than the act of killing itself. There is no question that news stations do need to report murders, robberies, fires, fatal crashes, and other stories about violence in their communities. The question is, to what degree and in what manner?

To help make right decisions, media look for help. Sometimes it comes from the people they cover. Portland, OR, TV and radio stations worked out an agreement with the city in 1998 in which police promised to provide tactical information and pool coverage access if the stations agreed not to broadcast information about police movements during hostage situations while the crisis is in progress. Under the agreement, stations can shoot as much video and record as much sound as they want, but must withhold it until the incident is resolved (Shepard, 2000).

Boston broadcast stations have made an agreement with law enforcement authorities to not broadcast pictures or sound of violent situations. In return, the police have pledged to give the cooperating stations a full and truthful account of the incident. At least one TV station refused to air a live picture of the Columbine shooting in Colorado because of that agreement, although it took place 2,000 miles from Boston.

During a hostage crisis in Baltimore, TV stations were both praised and criticized when they followed police recommendations in both reporting and withholding information during a lengthy standoff with a man believed to have killed four people, for fear the reports would agitate him (Trigoboff, 2000). Although the RTNDA Code of Ethics does not address violence, its published guidelines for covering hostage crises begins, "Always assume that the hostage taker, gunman or terrorist has access to the reporting." However, KCNC–TV news director Angie Kucharski pointed out that having guidelines is not the problem, the challenge is executing the plan.

Often news directors have legitimate reasons for their decisions, or reasons that seem logical at the time. The problem is, as Merrill (1997) pointed out, "the right" decision is not always obvious. The journalist may consult codes, develop a moral sense, find alternative possibilities for the actions, and even after that may still have doubts (Merrill, 1997).

One way to answer ethical criticism is to explain why a decision was made, the circumstances under which it was made, and the later evaluation of the decision. People watch TV news every day, and yet have little idea how the news process works, except as caricatured by television and movie fiction. Too often in response to criticism, broadcast journalists simply say, "We stand by our story." They fail to explain how the decision was reached or how the story was developed.

A Murderer on the Air, by Lee Hood

Should a journalistic organization help law enforcement do its job? Should a journalist accede to the demands of criminals? In the abstract, the answers would certainly be no. In the reality of a given situation, the answers are not so easy.

Such was the case of a Colorado Springs, CO, TV station's involvement in the apprehension of two fugitives in late January 2001. The two were the last of "The Texas Seven," who had escaped from a Texas prison in December and were suspected of killing a police officer near Dallas. After that, their whereabouts were unknown until someone in a small community near Colorado Springs recognized them from a report on "America's Most Wanted." Four were apprehended, one committed suicide, and two eluded police for several days, until they were cornered in a Colorado Springs motel room.

After hours of negotiations, the fugitives agreed to surrender but for one final request: a live interview on the local TV station they had been watching in their room. That station was the CBS affiliate, KKTV. News director Brian Rackham agreed to go talk to the officers involved in the negotiations. Once he was "thoroughly convinced" that the live interview was the only way to end the standoff, he gave the go-ahead. The interviewer would be Eric Singer, KKTV's main anchor, who was given no ground rules about what specific questions to ask, but was told to avoid "hot button questions" such as those involving the fugitives' escape or subsequent crimes.

Singer interviewed the fugitives via telephone, giving each 5 minutes of air time during which they gave rambling statements about the Texas prison system and answered Singer's questions about how they ended up in his community. The time was shortly after 3 a.m. After the interviews, the fugitives kept their word and surrendered peacefully. In their room afterward, police found a cache of loaded weapons.

Twelve hours later, a Denver, CO, TV reporter called to ask if I would agree to an interview about the ethics and propriety of what KKTV had done. The interviewer expressed surprise at my answers, apparently expecting an "ivory tower" response, an abstract answer that said journalists must never become an arm of law enforcement or a conduit for criminals. Instead, I said that being a journalist does not preclude one from being a citizen. I felt that the potential for a greater good outweighed the ethical concerns in this case.

The Poynter Institute, one of the most respected sources on journalistic ethics, criticized the station for violating the barriers between journalists and law enforcement. A Denver newspaper columnist criticized Singer as a "celebrity relay" for the fugitives, saying his role undermined his, and the media's, journalistic credibility.

Was the station helping law enforcement? Most certainly. Was the station allowing criminals a live, unedited forum for whatever they wanted to say? No question. Did the station become part of the news instead of just reporting it? No doubt, as evidenced by the number of national and local interviews Singer gave in the hours after the surrender.

But did the station also serve its community? For me this was the crucial question, and the answer was emphatically yes. TV stations are sometimes criticized for not doing enough to serve their communities, for caring more about profits than people. In this case, from my viewpoint, the people won. From the time we learned the fugitives were in Colorado, until the last two were captured, the entire state—and certainly the area around Colorado Springs—was on heightened alert. The remaining fugitives were known to be heavily armed, and their ring-leader, by then in jail, had admitted the group killed the officer in Texas. The TV station was given an opportunity to effect a peaceful surrender, relieving a nervous community and potentially saving lives, by offering unabridged air time at 3 o'clock in the morning. For me, there was very little harm, and a great deal of com-munity benefit, in the station cooperating.

Of the criticism he and the station received, news director Rackham told me, "I understand, in the world of theory, you don't want to be doing this." But he saw this case as a perfect example of why rules are made to be broken. And the com-munity benefit obviously weighed into his decision.

"We are citizens in this town, too," Rackham said.

Dan Dennison, news director at rival KOAA–TV, was critical of police for granting KKTV such extraordinary access behind police lines. But he was certain he would have made the same decision his counterpart, Brian Rackham, did.

"One of our roles is to be public servants, too," Dennison said. "Journalists sometimes forget that we're people first."

Dennison, like others, worries about the potential this incident has for inspiring copycats to seek out the media. That, indeed, is one argument for not acquiescing to criminals or anyone else seeking an open forum. But this was not a precedent-set-ting case. There have been such cases in the past, perhaps most famously the publi-cation of the Unabomber's manifesto several years ago. Shortly thereafter, Ted Kaczynski's brother recognized his writing and Kaczynski was arrested. Cases like this happen so infrequently that they become news when they do.

In my own research, my interviews with dozens of TV news viewers have made me realize many people feel a symbolic tie to local news. For me, this case was an opportunity to reflect on the different roles local news organizations fill in their communities, and perhaps to define them in a less restrictive way.

Lee Hood is a Broadcast News faculty member at the University of Colorado.

BOX 5.4

The news process remains a mystery to most of the audience, which draws its own conclusions, not always complimentary. A frequent response by jour-nalists when they are criticized for pandering to the public with violent con-tent is, "We're just giving the people what they want." However, ethics author Deni Elliot (1987) suggested that media are ducking the issue when they use that excuse. Journalists have the skill, knowledge, and responsibility to deter-mine what people need to know. "News media are not representative of the people's desires, they are professional interpreters of informational needs" (Elliot, 1987, p. 10). However, that power must be used judiciously. Ethical journalism is the result of the media realizing their power and their obligations (Elliot, 1987).

Journalists have an aversion to answering for their activities. RTNDA Chair-woman Barbara Cochran says traditionally, TV has done a poor job of explain-ing itself to the public (Heyboer, 1999). Even when the decision makers have considered the ethical implications of their actions, when it turns out wrong, people see it as a mistake instead of a decision made with deliberation.

And although one person—or even a group—may make an ethical decision on a story, that decision, in the confusion of deadlines, must be communicated to all. That obviously was not done in Denver, CO. In October 1999, a Denver station aired a story about a man who tied up rush hour traffic by lodging himself on a downtown statue, claiming he had dynamite strapped to his body. The decision was made, correctly, to withhold the person's name, and the reporter clearly stated it in his narrative. However, the person who edited the videotape apparently did not get the word. A document displayed on the screen clearly showed the man's name, at the very moment the reporter was saying that the name was being withheld. It not only shows the station as insensitive, but incompetent.

Media do not always use their freedoms well, raising the occasional call for some sort of mechanism to hold them accountable (Pritchard, 2000). One mechanism that journalists themselves have used is self-criticism, and one form of that is the journalism review (Bunton, 2000). However, in a study of journalism reviews, Bunton (2000) did not find much evidence of the impact of journalism reviews on the profession: "It is asserted, but rarely demonstrated" (Bunton, 2000, p. 72). Bunton studied the content of the *St. Louis Journalism Review* and found only 18 articles in 38 issues had media criticism as their primary theme, and "only 11 had reform as the dominant theme" (Bunton, 2000, p. 81). She also found that the *St. Louis Journalism Review* lacked influence with St. Louis journalists, and questioned the ability of the reviews to provide meaningful self-regulation.

There are several reasons why journalists need to be concerned with ethics. On a practical level, viewers are not usually idle and passive. They are thinking and reasoning human beings. They not only have opinions on whether ethically questionable material should be shown, they have an opinion on how a questionable story might be changed to make it acceptable (Lind, 1993). They are critical viewers.

Merrill (1997) gave two commonsense reasons why journalists should be ethical: a) because people in general are concerned about journalism ethics, and b) because journalists need the self-respect and satisfaction that comes from doing what is right. People, according to Merrill (1997), want journalism that is "dependable, credible, truthful, balanced, unbiased, thoughtful, interpretive, considerate, empathetic, and realistic" (p. 31).

Lambeth (1992) set out five principles to encourage ethical behavior: truthfulness, justice, freedom, humaneness, and stewardship. He said it is imperative that journalists develop the skills to achieve these principles. They must know how to be truthful, and how to dig for information they can present as truthful. They must know compassion and have a sense of morals. They must have the strength to remain free of outside influence. However, the responsibility does not lie solely with individual journalists. The companies they work for must be participants. The stations must encourage an atmosphere of truthfulness within the culture of the newsroom. The station must provide opportunities for reporters to hone their skills. The station must put humaneness over ratings so the journalist feels at liberty to leave out sensitive video or to cover a story with some sort of compassion both for the victims and the audience.

Compassion appeared to be lacking in a Dallas, TX, TV station's report of a 1999 shooting. A 13-year-old boy was shot by a 16-year-old boy who lived in the same house. The family was not named, although video of the house in a neighborhood of only 16 homes was shown, and the family was clearly identified as having recently moved from Alabama. At the end of the live story, the reporter said that police had not released the name of the 16-year-old who was being questioned because of juvenile protection laws, but neighbors told the reporter that the suspect was the brother of the victim. Although media are not prohibited from releasing such information, from an ethical point of view it is insensitive for the station to speculate, although it had fairly reliable information, or to identify the shooter when the police would not.

News directors should help their staffs sharpen their reporting and ethical skills by sending them to workshops, seminars, and conferences. The Poynter Institute, for example, has grown into one of the most prestigious and prominent schools for working journalists. It offers sessions in ethics, as well as various reporting skills. The RTNDA holds a 4-day annual convention, at which reporters can attend sessions on almost any aspect of broadcast journalism. The Society of Professional Journalists' annual convention covers all aspects of journalism. Regional workshops by RTNDA, the Society of Professional Journalists, and other organizations, give journalists even more opportunities to develop their skills.

As with most problems, that of the ethics of violence in TV news does not have just one cause. Other issues include the following:

- The technology to go live from virtually anywhere and get caught when a violent situation erupts.
- A lack of solid ethics background.
- Pressures to get the story first.
- Incessant deadlines.
- An emphasis on ratings.
- The newsroom or station atmosphere.
- Poor communication down the line once a decision is made.

CHAPTER SUMMARY

Ethics and media accountability issues are important in the study of crime coverage on local television news. The decisions that newsrooms make about the stories covered, lead material chosen, video used, and live shots planned, should be based on ethical principles and not simply business concerns. Often local television newsrooms face difficult decisions over the use of dramatic and violent video.

DISCUSSION QUESTIONS

1. Much of television reporting is done as teams of reporters, photographers, and sometimes producers. How would you assure that ethical decisions are made so that all viewpoints are heard? What should be the procedure to assure that everyone is aware of the decision?
2. Under what circumstances would you air video of a suicide? What are the reasons, both practical and ethical, for your decisions?
3. Many TV stations that show crime and violence in their newscasts say they are just giving the viewers what they want. Do you agree or disagree with that philosophy? Why?
4. If you were a television news director, how would you interpret the Society of Professional Journalists and RTNDA's Codes of Ethics that discourage the use of violent images on newscasts?
5. Your TV station has aired the story of the 16-year-old boy shooting a 13-year-old boy. Your reporter has said that although police are withholding the name of the 16-year-old, neighbors have said he's the brother of the victim. When a listener calls you, the news director, to complain, what will your reply be?

6

Coverage of the Courts,
Prisons, and Capital
Punishment

*"The corporate media, by willfully ignoring the dimensions today's prison crisis has
reached, is keeping the public uninformed, and in doing so subverting the public interest."*

—Daniel Burton-Rose, freelance journalist (1998, p. 29)

This chapter considers reporting of courthouse news, prison coverage, and capital punishment. The chapter examines why a few cases out of many attract attention of local TV newsrooms.

Dramatic events play an important role in attracting news reports about prisons and the death penalty:

> While few commentators mention how the media cover prisons, those who do generally agree on two critical points: that the press hardly attends to prison life at all and that what coverage there is usually concerns outbursts such as escapes and riots. (Lotz, 1991, p. 141)

In some cases, there is evidence that newspapers do a slightly better job than local television news of covering prisons. Although local television news departments frequently cover crime stories, they often ignore routine prison conditions. A prison riot, on the other hand, might be dramatic enough to warrant coverage. Likewise, the execution of a death row inmate is newsworthy. In some states, such as Florida and Texas, executions have become common occurrences. In other states, such as Nebraska and Minnesota, executions are rare or are not a legal option. This chapter examines local television news coverage of criminal punishment. Local television news is most likely to cover crimes as events that have just happened, and they sometimes cover the outcome of a case. But when it comes to the fate of criminals after sentencing, there is minimal coverage of inmates behind bars.

OUT OF SIGHT, OUT OF MIND

Local television news participates in the criminal process by its decision to pay attention to or ignore particular cases. Local television news is considered to be a main source of information, so a lack of coverage would limit what the public knows. In the broadest sense, society views the punishment of criminals as functional:

> It is a legal mechanism that allows us to take some of our fellow citizens and lock them in cages—or even kill them. Actually imposing such hard treatment on people typically curtails their liberty, stigmatizes and humiliates them, and makes them suffer. Merely the *threat* of such treatment, of course, limits the liberty of all citizens by making them afraid to engage in certain conduct. (Murphy, 1995, p. 1)

Some view harsh treatment in prison as valid because it is part of the punishment, and it serves societal notions of justice as defined by fairness: "Being first virtues of human activities, truth and justice are uncompromising" (Rawls, 1999, p. 4). It is possible, however, to view imprisonment as an ineffective and unfair deterrent:

> While the threat of a lengthy prison sentence is undoubtedly very effective at deterring white collar crimes that tend to be committed by middle class individuals, they are probably far less effective in deterring the crimes committed by underclass individuals, who are the primary occupants of prisons, and for whom the increment of pain associated with prison time may be far less severe than it would be for those ensconced in a comfortable job. (Blumstein, 1995, p. 417)

There is debate about the deterrent effect of imprisonment at a time when taxpayers face ever-increasing costs of prison operation. Today, the average annual cost per prisoner is about $20,000 (Blumstein, 1995, p. 416). Despite the dramatic growth in prison population during the last quarter century, the complex issues surrounding incarceration tend to be avoided by politicians and the news media:

> ... prisons have made the news in recent years because crowding and financial pressures have pushed them into the political and economic arenas. It is news when society runs out of space and starts diverting its unwanted to tin sheds, tents, barges, mess halls, and military bases. It is also news when new jails and prisons are built or planned. The usual response to them is "not in my backyard." (Lotz, 1991, pp. 155–156)

FIG. 6.1

Crime Stoppers began in Albuquerque, NM, in 1976. Citizens, media, and police forged a partnership in an effort to provide crime-solving assistance to law enforcement. A cash reward was offered to anonymous persons who telephoned the Crime Stoppers hot line with information that led to arrests and indictments. The Crime Stoppers program boasts an average conviction rate of 95% on cases solved by Crime Stoppers' tips. The Crime Stoppers programs worldwide have solved over a half a million crimes and recovered over 3 billion dollars worth of stolen property and narcotics. Today, there are over 1,000 Crime Stoppers programs in the United States, Canada, United Kingdom, Australia, South Africa, Bahamas, British West Indies, Micronesia, and other nations.

Crime Stoppers methods, objectives, successes, and phone numbers are publicized on a regular basis by the media. An unsolved "Crime of the Week" is given special treatment with details published in newspapers, on radio, and in certain cases a reenactment on television (Crime Stoppers, 2001).

In the case of local television news, some have criticized the involvement of law enforcement personnel in the news decision-making process. By becoming a part of the Crime Stoppers program, a local television station gives up some content control over a segment of its newscast. A second criticism of Crime Stoppers is the use of re-creations within a newscast when surveillance camera video is not available. Although having entertainment value, re-creations fall outside of the normal journalistic process of airing only actual footage. Often, Crime Stoppers segments use actors that fit suspect descriptions. If facts are missing, it is common to speculate about what might have happened. A third criticism is that many crimes featured by Crime Stoppers show minority suspects. The highly dramatic portrayal of crime scene re-creations may function to heighten fear about crime in a community.

BOX 6.1   Local TV News and Crime Stoppers.

Award-Winning Local Television News Reporter
Explains Prison Interview Difficulties

Mike McKnight is an investigative reporter with WOWT–TV in Omaha, NE. What follows is his description of how television reporters gain access to prisons and inmates.

He didn't speak, but his eyes called me vulture. Condemned murderer Harold "Walkin' Willie" Otey stood 10 feet away, and I listened as the deputy warden read his death warrant. Forty-five minutes later, I would watch him die in the electric chair. Probably because I was a witness to the execution, he never granted me an interview. But in 23 years, I've had my share of "one-on-ones" with killers. Some on death row, most doing life, and a few found not guilty by reason of insanity.

Every time it begins with a pat search followed by that walk through turnkey with the sounds of metal doors clanging shut. Usually an inmate or two yells, "Hey, I'm not guilty" or "The administration is violating my rights" or simply, "Look at my case." Everybody in prison is "innocent" or "abused by the system." Just ask them.

You approach a prison inmate or jail prisoner for an interview always knowing that nothing behind bars is free. I'm not talking about money changing hands. But whether spoken or not, the inmate will be asking, "What's in it for me?" That's where the reporter must become salesman.

First, start with jail or prison officials. Find out who would handle contact with an inmate and what are the institution's "rules" for an interview. In most facilities, if an inmate agrees to an interview, he has that right. However, wardens can require attorney approval. If a prison or jail official agrees to pass your request on to an inmate, leave a telephone number and time for a call back when you will be there to answer. Chances are it will be a collect call. If officials will not act as a go-between, then try to find the attorney representing the inmate. Most killers have ongoing appeals. Or, as an alternative you could write the inmate a letter, and enclose a self-addressed stamped envelope.

You know the opening line: "I want to tell your side of the story." But some inmates, especially in high-profile cases, know that you really want an exclusive. I always ask if there is a particular issue or passion they want others to hear about. Maybe it is religion or jailhouse lawyering or unfair shakedown searches of inmate cells. Remember, "What's in it for me?"

Although more difficult, even patients in mental institutions can be accessible to interviews. A family member is a good start there. But don't let it get you down if a door slams in your face. A psychiatrist working with a high-profile patient can also be a good start for an interview request. However, your reasons for the interview must be well thought out. Is there a certain type of therapy you can highlight? Remember, psychiatric professionals like their work publicized too. Or maybe the patient and doctor want to prove there is no danger in supervised excursions back into society. That sales pitch worked for me on a mother who murdered her four kids yet, after being found not guilty by reason of insanity, was released after therapy.

Correctional issues don't just involve inmate interviews. Prison staff have their own problems, from funding to training, although it may be tougher to get them on record because they all fear for their jobs. Union leaders and state senators with an interest in corrections can be good sources.

Believe me, if you develop a reputation as a journalist with an objective and fair interest in corrections, word will get around. Soon, those on the inside will be calling you with stories; usually collect.

Source: Mike McKnight, essay to authors, December 1999.

BOX 6.2

Mass media participate in promoting a view that stresses the need to be tough on criminals. Media attention that focuses on street gang crime and prison violence and riots tends to miss the larger context of the prison story (Jacobs, 1977). As a Chicago radio personality, who studied Illinois prisons, once observed, the public seems uninterested in knowing more about prisons:

Out of sight, out of mind; keep them there. That's where they belong, and don't let them out until their time is up. And, if they can readjust to society, fine. If not, throw them back in again. (Baum, in Lipschultz, 1980, p. 22)

Racism, by some accounts, helps explain why the prison problem is ignored. Civil rights leader Jesse Jackson believes that racial discrimination remains a part of American life: "... just as there are over one million blacks in college, there are more than one million in prison" (Jackson, 2000, p. 10). He cites high profile media cases such as the O. J. Simpson murder trial and the shooting of Amadou Diallo in New York as incidents that suggest that race is a "vexing" social problem.

It is fairly common for state and federal politicians to say they are "tough on crime," and for media, including local television news, to do "Crime Stoppers" features (Lavrakas, Rosenbaum,. & Lurigio, 1990).

The coverage of crime as a societal evil fits with news values. The complex issues of prisons and prisoners, however, do not lend themselves to brief sound bites. "It is important to find ways to remove prison policy from a primarily political agenda that reacts to the crime of the moment, and to develop a coherent schedule and process of imposing punishment and controlling offenders" (Blumstein, 1995, p. 417).

PRISON AND MEDIA ACCESS

One of the difficulties that local television newsrooms face in dealing with prison coverage is the lack of access to prison facilities. The courts have interpreted the First Amendment to guarantee a right to publish without governmental restraint, but the right to publication does not assure access to newsworthy information or places. A few local stations, most notably Northern California public television station KQED, have tested the limits. In the late 1970s, KQED sought access to the Alameda County Jail. In the end, the United States Supreme Court, in a split decision, found that media "… enjoys no special privilege of access beyond that which officials grant to the public in general" (Nelson & Teeter, 1986, p. 463). In the early 1990s, KQED wanted broadcast video of an execution at San Quentin. A federal district court ruled that the prison warden could restrict access: "Prohibition of cameras, still or television, from the execution witness area is a reasonable and lawful regulation" (*KQED v. Vasquez*, 1991, in Gillmor, Barron, & Simon, 1998, p. 435). Given the restricted access local television newsrooms face, it should not be surprising that prison coverage is sporadic.

In a handful of states, media access to prisoners for interviews has been banned. In a number of states, efforts are underway to make it more difficult for local news reporters to talk with prisoners.

> The CDC's [California Department of Corrections] attempt to shut out the media from the largest prison system in the world is part of a well-coordinated effort in several other states. California's regulations are closely monitored by other prison administrators because the state's prison rules are often used as a model for prison systems in the remainder of the country. (Wisely, 1998, p. 44)

As prison barriers to access are erected, the job of a local television news reporter wishing to do a story about a prisoner or prison life becomes more difficult.

PRISON RIOTS MAKE NEWS

One exception to the general rule that prisons tend not to be covered by local television news is the prison riot. In cases where inmates have rioted, injured, or killed other inmates or guards, or disrupted routine prison operations, journalists tend to see news value. For local television news, the prison riot lends itself to live shots. It is a breaking story involving safety in the community, law enforcement, weapons, and drama. In some cases, a hostage crisis unfolds. News live trucks and helicopters can be sent to the scene to provide immediate coverage of the event as it happens.

During the 1990s, prison disturbances continued to be newsworthy. For example, in October of 1995 a riot at a federal prison in Talladega, AL, became a local and national story. WBRC's Antoyne Green told CNN that six guards were injured in a prison with a history of disturbances:

> Now police, as you can probably hear, helicopters are still in the air and police are still searching the area for possible escapees…. Now, when we first arrived here

More than 4,200 people have been executed via the electric chair in the United States. The electric chair originally was considered more humane than public hangings. At issue today is whether the electric chair is a painful means of taking a condemned killer's life. Following is a listing of some of the key developments in the adoption and decline of the use of the electric chair:

- 1881—The electric chair is proposed by a Buffalo, NY, dentist. He was inspired by an accidental, and apparently painless, death.
- 1888—New York became the first state to adopt the electric chair as its means of capital punishment.
- 1890—New York performed the first execution by electric chair.
- 1923—Florida's "Old Sparky" electric chair was built by inmates.
- 1972—The U.S. Supreme Court's *Furman v. Georgia* decision struck down the death penalty as unconstitutional.
- 1976—In the *Gregg v. Georgia* decision, the Supreme Court ruled that rewritten state death penalty laws are constitutional. At the same time, states begin to move toward lethal injection as the means of execution.
- 1979—Electric chair executions resume for the first time since 1972.
- 1990—A botched electric chair execution in Florida prompted public controversy.
- 1999—A new electric chair in Florida failed to quell public concerns about electrocutions. The Supreme Court agreed to consider whether the electric chair should be outlawed as "cruel and unusual punishment."
- 2000—Florida shifted to lethal injection. The two remaining states using the electric chair, Alabama and Nebraska, considered ending the practice in favor of lethal injection. In May, a district judge in Nebraska ruled that the method used—three pauses between four jolts of electricity—was cruel and unusual punishment. At the same time, New Hampshire's governor promised to veto a bill that would repeal the death penalty—something no state has done since the U.S. Supreme Court reinstated capital punishment. In Illinois, the governor suspended all executions pending a study. Thirteen death row inmates in that state were released after it was learned they were either wrongly or unfairly convicted.

Sources: John Cook, *Mother Jones, 25,* p. 27; Robynn Tysver, "Execution method rejected," *Omaha World-Herald,* May 8, 2000, p. 13; Leslie Reed, "Anti-execution push parallels Nebraska's," *Omaha*

BOX 6.3   A Brief History of the Electric Chair in the United States.

about maybe three hours ago, ambulances and emergency crews were consistently streaming down the road, trying to get into the prison. Otherwise, all of the roads leading up to the prison were blocked off. (Cable News Network, 1995)

In another riot, a violent clash occurred between Hispanic American and African American inmates at the New Folsom Prison in California in September 1996. One inmate died, and 13 others were injured. CNN reporter Greg Lefevre emphasized prison overcrowding and racial tensions:

It happened here, the exercise yard at the new maximum-security Folsom prison—violence between black and Hispanic inmates.... Guards used pepper spray, then batons, rubber bullets, then live, lethal ammunition. They fired at least fourteen times.... This fight may have been anticipated, or even planned. Guards found inmates armed with knives, fingernail clippers and sharpened toothbrushes.... Problems between Blacks and Hispanics here are made worse by overcrowding. More than 3,000 inmates live here—nearly twice as many as the 1,700 it's supposed to hold. (Cable News Network, 1996)

As is often the case with such live and breaking news, networks such as CNN first rely on retransmission of local station broadcasts, sometimes follow with local reporter stand-ups and packages, and may send a CNN reporter to the scene for follow-up and ongoing coverage. CNN, in this case, interviewed then California Governor Pete Wilson, who said the fight was between two prison gangs, and that it was racially organized. Beyond prison riot coverage, there has been some local television news coverage of gang-related crimes said to be directed by gang leaders from behind the walls of prisons. Just as prison riots or gang-related crime lead to local news coverage, so too does the prospect of a state-sponsored execution. Death penalty cases are seen by newsrooms as dramatic news events that warrant substantial coverage.

MASS MEDIA AND THE DEATH PENALTY

The death penalty in general, and execution by electric chair in particular, produces a difficult set of circumstances for local television news. On the one hand, television news is called on to cover, and even to treat as normal, death penalty procedures of the state. On the other hand, electric chair executions are viewed by many as inhumane and a painful death (Freedburg, 1997). In a recent Gallup Poll, 51% of Americans said the death penalty is applied fairly in the United States, but 41% believe it is applied unfairly. Two thirds of Americans, 66%, support the death penalty. Support has declined in recent years from a high of 80% in 1994 (Jones, 2000).

Invented more than 100 years ago, the electric chair was originally seen "as a quick and painless execution method after witnesses were shocked by hangings that went awry" (Freedburg, 1997, p. A1). However, a botched electric chair execution in Florida in 1997 added to the debate over whether the chair in states where it is mandated should be replaced by lethal injection (Clary, 1997).

There is extensive research on the death penalty, but little research connecting it to the mass media. By the late 1960s, about 1 in 10 convicted murderers was sentenced to death (Stevens, 1978). This was a change from the perception of justice in 1791, when the Eighth Amendment was adopted. At that time "a death sentence was imposed without questions on every person convicted of a capital offense" (Stevens, 1978, p. 10). From 1930 to 1967, an average of more than 100 U.S. executions were carried out each year (Carelli, 1997). A brief Supreme Court moratorium in the early 1970s followed.

The reinstatement of the death penalty in 1976 led to only six executions through 1982 (Boellstorff, 1996). During the late 1970s and 1980s the U.S. Supreme Court defined capital defendants' rights and encouraged "expeditious executions" (White, 1991, p. 5). The number of executions in the United States since 1982 has risen steadily from five in 1983 to 74 in 1997—the most since 1955 (Carelli, 1997).

By the early 1990s, significant changes in the capital punishment system led scholars to predict that the number of executions would increase in all regions of the country (White, 1991). There seems to be agreement among death penalty scholars that public opinion polls reflect consistent support for capital punishment. In a 1977 survey, for example, 40% of respondents supported mandatory capital punishment in all first-degree murder cases. Another 44% said it depends on the circumstances. Only 13% rejected the death penalty (Vidmar & Ellsworth, 1982, p. 89). Support for the death penalty climbed during the 1980s, and is at its highest point since the beginning of modern polling in 1952 (Costanzo & Costanzo, 1994, p. 249). Although support for the death penalty has climbed over the years, between 1974 and 1994 there was a consistent "gender gap" with men more likely than women to support executions (Andersen, 1997, p. 28). Public attitudes toward capital punishment are seen as "expressions of intense anger toward violent criminals" (Costanzo & Costanzo, 1994, p. 252).

Gitlin (1980) pointed out almost 2 decades ago that television is a magnifying glass for American society. On live television, "visual simultaneity provides a dimension of experience that is like being transported to the scene" (Lang & Lang, 1984, p. 26). As we discussed earlier in this book, crime news—and specifically executions—can be viewed from a social construction of reality perspective. Local television news may be assumed to be better than "being there" (Lang & Lang, 1984).

Studies of media and crime, even the most recent research, mention the death penalty in passing, if at all (Bailey & Hale, 1998). Research on the sociology of news work, as it relates to local television, has identified two key generalizations: (a) local news tends to rely on "routine" sources, including government officials and law enforcement personnel (Reese & Buckalew, 1995); and (b) competitive and corporate interests appear to "help *homogenize* the news rather than *diversify* it" (Ehrlich, 1995, p. 205). In the case of local TV news coverage of executions, the selection of the same sources will lead to consonance in coverage. Given the dramatic nature of the conflict between proponents and opponents of capital punishment, local television news stations are faced with a difficult choice. Either they report live from the prison showing scenes of conflict between demonstrators, or they cover the story using in-studio experts for analysis and avoid the location where the news was taking place.

The literature on local television news has been limited in addressing how local television covers an execution. Although political scientist Doris Graber (1997) devoted a chapter in one of her books to news coverage of the justice system, she did not discuss media coverage of executions. Graber wrote that organizational factors are important in determining news making and reporting routines:

> Colleagues and settings strongly influence news people. Every news organization has its own internal power structure that develops from the interaction of owners, journalists, news sources, audiences, advertisers, and government authorities. In most news organizations today, the internal power structure is slightly left of middle America, yet predominantly supportive of the basic tenets of the current political and social system. (Graber, 1997, p. 96)

Detweiler (1987) explored journalists' views on executions. He found strong agreement among journalists that "Those who use the site of an execution to raise the public consciousness for or against the issue of capital punishment are an important part of the story" (p. 456). These journalists also agreed that official state sources were only half the story of an execution. The journalists disagreed with the statement that "Reporters should not cover demonstrations at the site of executions which are obviously staged to attract the media" (p. 456).

Capital punishment demonstrators may create newsworthy events that "stress emotion and drama" (Kaniss, 1991, p. 109). An execution fits models of local newsworthiness by focusing on the actions of government and the issue of crime. The focus on tragedies of victims and personalities of the condemned killers help local TV news bring a human angle to the execution story. The death penalty "represents stories that society tells about itself, stories that tend to reflect key ideological beliefs of society" (Berkowitz, 1997, p. 499). At the same time, sensationalized coverage of an execution scene fits the market-driven "local television news formula" of the 1990s (Underwood, 1998, p. 171).

The mass media seem to be a major source of information people use to develop views about such social issues as the death penalty. "In this way, the media have played an indirect but significant long-term role in shaping people's thoughts and actions" (DeFleur & Dennis, 1996, p. 595). Where media messages are consonant, it is possible that the content will have the effect of influencing people (Noelle-Neumann, 1995).

ace in dealing with prison coverage is the lack of access to prison
s. One exception to the general rule that prisons tend not to be covered
television news is the prison riot. In cases where inmates have rioted,
or killed other inmates or guards, or disrupted routine prison opera-
urnalists tend to see news value. The death penalty in general, and exe-
by electric chair in particular, however, produces a difficult set of
tances for local television news. The transition from electric chair to le-
ection as the preferred method of execution created a less dramatic
r local television news. In the end, news media largely ignore the pun-
t and corrections components of the criminal justice system.

DISCUSSION QUESTIONS

o you believe that a story about corrections in your city must have dra-
atic events to be newsworthy?
ow might local news reporters work to improve access to prison facilities
r routine coverage? Are there news values in such efforts?
a prison riot, what are some of the difficulties faced by newsroom per-
nnel in covering the story?
hat are some of the potential headaches associated with live coverage
om the scene of an execution?
a your opinion should executions be televised? What journalistic issues
rface from such coverage?

It has been argued that the mass media are willing ⸻
cial myths:

> The social construction of myths of crime and criminal ⸻
> series of recurrent patterns. These patterns allow for an u⸻
> social attention to be focused upon a few isolated crimi⸻
> attention is promoted by intense, but often brief, mass n⸻
> problem. (Kappeler et al., 1993, pp. 4–5)

This idea is related to the view that mass media portra⸻
ity for individuals and groups. Surette (1992) argued t⸻
prisons and prisoners is shaped by entertainment portr⸻
appeals to "voyeuristic instincts" (pp. 41, 74). Ultima⸻
ports law-and-order policies and becomes "the accep⸻
ity" (p. 76). Social construction of reality began witl⸻
that "all symbolic universes and all legitimations are h⸻
istence has its base in the lives of concrete individuals,⸻
tus apart from these lives" (Berger & Luckmann, 196⸻
more recent times, has been linked to research on te⸻
(1984), as mentioned earlier, generalized that local tel⸻
close-up views, live event coverage, video, and ongoi⸻

As Surette (1998) observed, news media largely ignore⸻
rections components of the criminal justice system: "In⸻
tioned directly so infrequently in the news that content ⸻
corrections are rare" (p. 70). Death penalty cases and pr⸻
routine events do not: "When a news story does deal wit⸻
ways reports its subject in a negative light or deals not dir⸻
with an execution or a riot" (p. 70). Even in events drama⸻
cal television news coverage, impact on the public rema⸻

> It is well established that media coverage can affect the p⸻
> policies and events. It is less clear, however, that these ⸻
> deeply felt beliefs or that they are long lasting. Public opir⸻
> times, turn a deaf ear to the most sensational media events⸻
> tween a news story, public opinion and policy change is dif⸻
> it is merely assumed. (Doppelt & Manikas, 1990, p. 129)

Local television newsrooms are attracted to stories tha⸻
prison riot or impending execution, but they rarely eve⸻
tions might be covered under normal circumstances.

CHAPTER SUMMARY

Dramatic events play an important role in attracting n⸻
ons and the death penalty. One of the difficulties that⸻

7

Case Study:
Three Nebraska Executions

"There is an out-of-town station that is parked right in front of the crowd, the pro-execution crowd, and the lights they have shining on them and the live shots they are doing are kind of inciting the crowd a little bit."

—Carol Schrader, Omaha, NE, news anchor (1996)

Any investigation of crime and local television news coverage must include an examination of the ultimate punishment—the death penalty. This chapter looks at the evolution of local TV coverage of capital punishment in one state. The focus is on the portrayal of the executions of Harold Otey, John Joubert, and Robert Williams, by four Omaha, NE, television stations. Local television coverage of an execution scene is a social construction of reality, shaped by the social conflict of symbols, actors, and meanings, and influenced by journalistic decision making that tends to create a consonant view among mass media. These three executions provide a particularly clear window into the nature of local television news. On the nights that Otey and Joubert were executed, Omaha television stations portrayed the social conflict between supporters and opponents of capital punishment and emphasized the death penalty as appropriate justice.

Although much is known about the justice and injustice of capital punishment, little has been written about the role that local television news organizations play in the public's perception of the death penalty. The case of Harold Otey provided an opportunity to examine the role of local television in a state where 35 years had elapsed between executions. The case of John Joubert provided an opportunity to study a second modern-day execution. The case of Robert Williams was an opportunity to further study the content of live television broadcasts.

Before discussing media coverage of executions during the 1990s, it is important to look back at a high profile case in the early days of local television news. Shortly after midnight on June 25, 1959, Charles Starkweather died in Nebraska's electric chair. He had been convicted for the murder of a teenager, and accused of 10 other homicides. Most of those homicides occurred within a 72-hr period in January 1958 in and around Lincoln, NE. Starkweather was the 20th person executed in Nebraska since the state took over these duties from the counties in 1901. Eight of the 20 were hanged until the electric chair was chosen as the method of execution in 1913. Local television stations in Omaha had covered the Starkweather story from the beginning (Hilt, 1990). By the time Starkweather was arrested in Wyoming and brought to the state penitentiary in Lincoln, local and network television crews were waiting for him. Intense television coverage continued through the Starkweather execution. "The public in the late 1950s watched television news with a fascination that it does not have today, and because the medium itself was still new, the television audience easily could be swept up in the program, whether it was entertainment or news" (Hilt, 1990, p. 3). The highly dramatic nature of the crime story led it to be among the first to receive nationwide television exposure. Journalists who covered the case said that there appeared to be no opposition to the imposition of the death penalty on Starkweather (Hilt, 1990).

The case study in this chapter involved qualitative analysis of the coverage of the three executions by four Omaha television stations. Bogdan and Biklen (1992) defined this type of qualitative research as describing processes in the inductive search for meaning. Additionally, the cultural studies approach searches for "the intersection of social structure and human agency" (p. 41). This examination looks at local television news content as symbolic cultural messages that create "meanings" (McQuail, 1994, p. 94). Constructed meanings are powerful and subjective social realities grounded in the language of human culture (DeFleur & Ball-Rokeach, 1989, pp. 250–262). As such, local television news is defined as the product of "dramatic actors," with the actors being the news makers, the news sources, and the news deliverers (Bennett, 1996, pp. 52–53). Off-air recordings were made of each of the station's late newscasts and special live coverage.

OTEY: THE FIRST NEBRASKA EXECUTION IN 35 YEARS

On Friday, September 2, 1994, Harold Lamont "Walkin' Willie" Otey died in Nebraska's electric chair. Otey was one of 31 death row inmates nationwide to be executed in 1994. At 12:40 a.m. the Associated Press sent this "bulletin" to its Nebraska broadcast affiliates: "Harold Lamont Otey died in the electric chair early Friday for the rape and murder of a woman 17 years ago." In the "urgent" that followed seconds later, the state newswire added that Otey was the first to die in Nebraska's electric chair since Charles Starkweather was executed in 1959.

In contrast to mass media coverage of the Starkweather crime spree, the crime Otey was convicted of did not attract nationwide news coverage. Otey was sentenced to death in 1978 for the rape and murder of 26-year-old Jane McManus in 1977. Although the crime itself was an Omaha story, Otey's numerous last-minute death penalty appeals attracted the attention of the CBS news magazine "48 Hours." The Otey case came to symbolize public frustration with a justice system that took 16 years to execute a condemned killer.

The four Omaha television stations began their late evening newscasts on September 1, 1994, with the latest information on the upcoming execution of Otey. Official state sources and death penalty supporters and opponents dominated the live coverage of the execution. Of the four Omaha television stations, CBS affiliate KMTV was most dramatic in its 10 p.m. lead: "This is a live picture of the Nebraska State Penitentiary. A cool, overcast night that condemned killer Harold Otey wishes would never end." A brief sampling of each station's coverage shows how the event was framed:

- KPTM (9 p.m.)—The FOX affiliate aired two reporter packages, one from the prison and one from a gathering of death penalty opponents. Reporter Will Jamison interviewed death penalty opponent DeKoursey Spiker at an all-day vigil at the Nebraska Governor's mansion in Lincoln. Spiker said, "I feel a frenzy of desire for an execution. And the pain that people who oppose the execution have had to go through, and the family and friends of the person ... it has not made our state a better place."
- KETV (10 p.m.)—The ABC affiliate reported that the crowd gathered well before the scheduled execution time. The station featured an interview with John Breslow, state auditor and official observer. Breslow said, "Just as I happened to walk in, he (Otey) walked out of the visitor's room, and he looked at me and says 'Breslow, what's going on,' or 'what's happening' or something like that, and I said 'Nothing, have you heard anything?' And he said, 'Yeah, 6–2' and then put his thumb down and that was it. And then they started doing his last will." Reporter John Croman was live with demonstrators outside the penitentiary. He estimated that there were about 100 people on each side of the issue. The video showed antideath penalty teenagers with signs that read, "Give him life not death!!! He too has the right to live." Croman followed with the comment, "We get anything from 'Fry Willie' to peace signs back to us."
- WOWT (10 p.m.)—The NBC affiliate began with anchor Gary Kerr live at the prison. This station aired the same sound bite of John Breslow that was aired by competitor KETV. The station invited legal expert James Martin Davis to their newsroom: "That's probably the longest clemency appeal in a death row case that I think has ever been perpetrated in the history of the country." Investigative reporter Mike McKnight was also one of five media witnesses (there were 10 in all) for the execution. Anchor Pat Persaud reported live from the home of the family of the victim,

TABLE 7.1

Organizational News Gathering Routines in the Late Night Newscast
Coverage of the Three Nebraska Executions, and the Late Morning Live
Coverage of the Williams Execution[**]

	KPTM	KETV	WOWT	KMTV
Anchor(s) at prison		A, B, D	A, B, D	A, B, D
Reporter(s) at prison with demonstrators	A, C	A, B, D	A, B, D	A, B, C
Live at prison		A, B, D	A, B, D	A, B, D
Reporter(s) with governor	A	B, D		B
Reporter(s) at state capitol		A, B		A
Reporter(s) at attorney general's office	B	A	B	B
Reporter(s) with victim's family	C	C, D	A, B, C, D	A, C, D
Reporter inside prison (telephone)	B, C	B, D	A, B, D	B
Prerecorded interview with condemned man		B, C	A, C	A, B, C
Interview with state observer		A	A	A
Interview with prison officials		A, B, C, D	B, D	A
Interview with execution witnesses	C	A, B, C, D	A, B, D	B, C

(continued on next page)

	KPTM	KETV	WOWT	KMTV
Interview with defense attorneys	A, B	A, D	A, B	
On-set interview with legal experts		B, D	A, D	B
Person on the street		B, D		
Interview with others (ethicist, boyfriend of victim)	B	A, B, D	B, D	A, B

Note. **A denotes Otey execution coverage; B denotes Joubert execution coverage; C denotes Williams execution coverage; D denotes live coverage of Williams execution.

Jane McManus. This report included a sound bite from the victim's mother: "To have Jane's picture out there so that other people in their minds, they can see Jane too, and know that she was a vibrant young girl that was slaughtered."

- KMTV (10 p.m.)—Anchors Loretta Carroll and John Mason reported live from the prison. This station also used the sound bite from John Breslow aired on KETV and WOWT. Reporter Mary Williams was live at the McManus house. Reporter Deborah Ward was live at the prison with opponents of the death penalty. She included a shouting match between people on both sides of the death penalty issue:

Opponent: "None of you are about productivity, you're all about killing others. You think killing is going to solve everything. You kill Otey, crime goes down. Well it doesn't."

Proponent: "Why don't you sit on his lap?"

Opponent: "Why? You want me dead too. That's wonderful. This gentleman over here wants me to die for saying something. That's absolutely wonderful. And these young men right here think this is a barbecue. They're cannibals."

Ward reported that one of the largest signs said, "Welcome to the Nebraska State Pen's First Annual Barbecue."

The organizational news gathering routines of all the stations were similar in that they relied on most of the same sources, and reported from most of the same places.

The anchors and reporters for all four stations engaged in interpretation of the events going on around them. What follows is a sampling of the broadcast journalists' construction of the "reality" outside the Nebraska State Penitentiary:

- John Croman, KETV—"Prison officials have a system here. They're going to keep the antideath penalty people in this pen over here, and they've got the prodeath penalty people set to go here in this pen, and in the middle, right here, you have sort of a demilitarized zone to try to keep the two sides apart. And you could see the need for that separation when members of the Lincoln Prayer Circle encountered a large group of Lincoln East High School football players" (shouting between the two groups).
- Gary Johnson, WOWT—"Many feel their convictions so strongly that they've come out here tonight to make a stand. And while there are many law enforcement personnel out here tonight to make sure everything goes right, and I haven't seen any violence, but already the shouting matches have begun.... Lincoln tonight is a city of extremes. Earlier I drove by a residence where they were having a party in favor of the death penalty complete with banners for decorations and a mock electric chair. Just to my left where those protesting the death penalty are, they're lighting candles. Several people are already weeping, and they're waving to Harold Otey, who's looking out of the penitentiary at his onlookers tonight."
- Deborah Ward, KMTV—"The screaming is expected to continue through the night, off and on. Right now it's quiet. A lot of the people out here, however, are kids. It's kind of like Dodge Street [a main Omaha road] at the height of cruising. And businesses right across the street from the prison are now trying to profit off the execution."

Three of the four Omaha television stations aired special reports following 10 o'clock newscasts. KETV went live to the penitentiary, referring to the "carnival atmosphere" as demonstrators from both sides of the issue shouted at each other across a "demilitarized zone." The station highlighted the interplay between the demonstrators, and showed that the two groups were separated by two snow fences a few feet apart. They showed this at about the time of the scheduled execution (12:01 a.m.), as the crowd chanted "Joubert's next, Joubert's next." The crowd also chanted "Hey, hey, goodbye."

WOWT showed Otey waving from a prison hospital window. The station chose to avoid showing the crowd by not showing video of the gathering. However, the crowd could be heard in the background. KMTV described the scene as having a "carnival atmosphere" and called the demonstrators "boisterous protesters." In-studio guest and former Otey attorney, Douglas County public defender Tom Riley, called the scene outside the prison "disturbing and terrible":

Look what's going on out there. We're supposed to be a civilized society. We got people standing out there with nonsensical signs, screaming back and forth at each other. This is what people want as justice? This is absurd.

The station attempted to connect the Otey execution with the Starkweather execution by interviewing former television reporter Ninette Beaver: "I don't think anybody really opposed the execution of Charlie Starkweather, or very few. We didn't have 17 years of appeals; he was executed within 17 months." Generally, "television's portrayal of the execution of Harold Otey shied away from the complexities of the death penalty issue by emphasizing the most dramatic aspects of the evening" (Lipschultz & Hilt, 1998, p. 29).

JOUBERT: CHILD KILLER PUT TO DEATH

On Wednesday, July 17, 1996, the death penalty was enforced on John Joubert. At 12:29 a.m. the Associated Press sent this to its Nebraska broadcast affiliates: "John Joubert was put to death in Nebraska's electric chair for butchering two boys in an Omaha suburb 13 years ago" (Howard, 1996). Joubert was sentenced to death for killing 13-year-old Danny Jo Eberle and 12-year-old Christopher Walden in 1983. This case combined elements of the Starkweather and Otey crimes: a manhunt for the killer, heightened public fears, and ultimately public frustration with the justice system.

It would be nearly 2 years before Omaha television stations again confronted the coverage of an execution. In July of 1996, John Joubert received the death penalty. The state of Nebraska made three obvious adjustments in the wake of the Otey execution: (a) the gap was widened between demonstrators, (b) law enforcement agencies increased their presence outside the prison, and (c) Governor Ben Nelson urged citizens to stay away. Despite these measures, the crowd for the Joubert execution appeared to be as large and boisterous (particularly the prodeath penalty side) as the crowd for the Otey execution. Television stations were faced with a similar crowd scene as the backdrop for live coverage beginning with their late newscasts. On this particular evening, severe weather coverage and a major Omaha redevelopment plan voted on by the county commission competed for airtime:

- KPTM (9 p.m.)—The station chose to lead with a tornado warning issued for counties in the northern part of the viewing area, and then went to the Joubert execution story. The story began with each anchor reading a sentence: (a) Byron Wood— "As it stands now, the state of Nebraska will carry out its next execution in about 3 hours;" (b) Coanchor Lisa Volenec—"Condemned child killer John Joubert is scheduled to die in Nebraska's electric chair just after midnight for the 1983 murders of two Sarpy County boys." The station then went to a telephone report from reporter Jackie Madara, who summarized the situation in Lincoln.

- KETV (10 p.m.)—Spot weather news led this newscast. The station then began its coverage of the Joubert execution with coanchor Carol Schrader saying, "He's confessed to killing two Sarpy County boys." The station then aired an audio tape of Joubert: "When I pulled out the knife he said please don't kill me!" Schrader continued: "Tonight John Joubert is just hours away from his execution." This was followed by reporter Julie Cornell explaining the changes at the penitentiary following the Otey execution: "You'll remember the Governor and many Nebraskans were appalled by the behavior of the folks out here at the Otey execution. Tonight, the Governor asked folks to respect each other, if they come out here and keep their cool." The story included a sound bite from Governor Ben Nelson: "This is neither the time nor the place for an inappropriate atmosphere as we experienced nearly 2 years ago." Cornell's story continued by showing the penitentiary, where blinds covered the windows of the infirmary. Prison officials did not want Joubert to be seen by the demonstrators or the media, as had happened when Otey waved to the crowd.

The station discussed crowd control at the prison. Security was seen as tighter, and law enforcement personnel did not allow demonstrators on the property until after 10:30 p.m. The anchors and reporters compared the crowd at the Joubert execution to that at the Otey execution. The widened gap between demonstrators was not large enough to prevent the proponents and opponents of the death penalty from hearing each other and yelling responses. Death penalty proponents displayed signs similar to those at the Otey execution, such as, "Wire the chair to a dimmer switch and roll it SLOWLY!" and "Thank God for electricity." The crowd played to the television cameras when lights went on, and KETV did not resist showing the intensity of the moment.

- WOWT (10 p.m.)—The newscast began with the Joubert execution story. Coanchor Don Hudson opened the newscast by saying, "Nothing appears to be standing in the way for John Joubert's execution." Coanchor Pat Persaud added, "And here is the up-to-the-minute update. All of Joubert's appeals have been exhausted." The station then went to reporter Amy Adams, who was in the crowd: "It is becoming a circus atmosphere." The station reported that events outside the penitentiary were not working as state officials had hoped. However, compared with the coverage on KETV, WOWT described rather than showed the "raucous activity."
- KMTV (10 p.m.)—This station also led with the Joubert execution story. Coanchor Michael Scott began the newscast by saying, "In a little more than 2 hours, John Joubert will pay for his crimes with his life. This time, no court will step in and save him." The station then ran a story contrasting the Otey execution. This station also used a sound bite from Gover-

nor Nelson: "I would prefer that there be no crowds there but recognizing that there are likely to be crowds, I hope that they would respect one another and that decorum will be the order of the evening." Reporter Deborah Ward was amid the crowd outside the penitentiary: "The buffer zone does appear to be helping. While there is still yelling, in fact there was a smoke bomb thrown just seconds ago, it is somewhat quieter than when Harold Lamont Otey was executed." Mark Pettit, former KMTV anchor and author of a book on the Joubert case (1990), was at the prison as the crowd become more unruly: "It's an argument not to have, I guess, this kind of build-up around an execution. You want to make it as public as possible, I think, to make people understand how the system works, but as you see what happened here it has built into a little bit of a frenzy." The live coverage for KETV, WOWT, and KMTV followed the late night newscasts. The stations followed the structure of the Otey live coverage and the content of the Joubert 10 p.m. reports.

WILLIAMS: NEBRASKA LEARNS ITS LESSON

On Tuesday, December 2, 1997, Robert E. Williams died in the electric chair. Long before the execution, he had confessed to murdering three women during a 3-day crime spree in 1977. Associated Press reporter Robynn Tysver wrote the following: "His execution was the first daytime execution and the first to be witnessed by a victim's relative in Nebraska since the state resumed carrying out the death penalty in 1994" (Tysver, 1997, p. 13). The Williams execution in 1997 was one of 74 across the country, more than in any of the past 42 years (Carelli, 1997), and the most since the age of television. The Williams case differed from the previous executions in that the news media did not portray it as dramatically as they had the other crimes. Williams was a confessed killer who did not resist or challenge the death penalty sentence.

Once again, Nebraska officials made dramatic changes in the execution procedure: (a) the execution was scheduled for 10 a.m., the first daytime execution in the state; (b) the gap between opponents and proponents of the death penalty was further widened to the point that the two groups could not hear one another; and (c) Governor Ben Nelson again urged citizens to stay away from the penitentiary. The changes worked, because the crowd was significantly smaller and less boisterous than before. Television coverage followed the lead of the state, and played down the execution. Although the execution was still a lead story, it no longer dominated the broadcasts.

The live coverage of the Williams execution occurred between 10 and 11 in the morning. The most extensive coverage came from KETV, which began at 10 a.m. and lasted for more than 1 hr. Anchor Rob McCartney mentioned how the scene outside the prison was calmer than during the previous two executions: "Right now it is very quiet and very calm, unlike the executions that have taken place in the last 3 years with Harold Otey and John Joubert, where as we all know, the situation got a little out of hand, a little out of control. Things right now at the penitentiary are pretty calm." While he was saying this, the station showed a lone death penalty proponent who quietly stood, displaying a sign that read "Uphold the law! Fry the BASTARD." Later in the live report, after word that the execution had been carried out, KETV played a story pointing out the differences between the Otey, Joubert, and Williams executions by showing footage of the conflict during the Joubert execution. A death penalty opponent said that the state was trying to "normalize" capital punishment by moving the execution to daylight hours. Reporter Pamela Jones was asked whether she saw any problems between opponents and proponents waiting outside the penitentiary: "There weren't any problems that we could recognize. There were only people who were trying to disperse some of the supporters after everything was over with."

By comparison, the other stations had limited live coverage. In the case of the FOX affiliate KPTM, there was no live coverage. WOWT began its live coverage at 10 a.m. Anchor Gary Kerr was live outside the penitentiary, and he pointed out that there were more news people present than demonstrators. Kerr said there was none of the "hoopla" that was present at the earlier executions. Their coverage focused on live telephone reports from inside the prison, a package summarizing Williams' crimes, another package discussing the lethal injection versus electrocution issue, and videotape of the witnesses' news conference. WOWT interrupted programming to deliver the news concerning the Williams execution, but did not provide continuous coverage. Their two updates each ran about 10 min. KMTV had two brief live reports from their anchors outside the penitentiary. The first report included a sound bite from a victim's husband. The second report included a debriefing with their reporter who had been inside the penitentiary.

- KPTM (9 p.m.)—The station emphasized how different the scene outside the penitentiary was compared with the scenes during the Otey and Joubert executions. The station included sound bites with opponents and proponents of the death penalty. The tone of the comments reinforced the station's assertion that this was a "kinder, gentler" group. "I don't believe in the antics of the people in the past at night where they were drunk and yelling obscenities at people against the death penalty. That's not right. Everyone is entitled to their opinion," said one proponent of the death penalty.
- KETV (10 p.m.)—Nearly 12 hr after the execution, Robert Williams' final statement and reporter Brad Stephens' eyewitness account were the new elements during KETV's late newscast. A major theme of the coverage was that Williams was ready to die. Witness Bill Hord said, "It was a very polite atmosphere, and I agree that Mr. Williams helped to set that tone, and if he was looking for the grace to get through this, I

would say he found it." KETV reporter Brad Stephens was one of 10 witnesses to the execution. He reported on Williams' final statement: "I just appreciate livin' long enough to be blessed by so many people that God has let into my life and my last statement would be that I hope this incident will inspire other people to find another way.... I'm on my way home. Thank you." The station estimated that there were about 100 demonstrators, but that the scene was much calmer than previous executions. Although KETV was live from the prison scene in the morning, by the late-night newscast the only live coverage was the in-studio interview with their reporter who witnessed the execution.

- WOWT (10 p.m.)—This station led its late-night newscast with a package concerning a drug sniffing dog demonstration. The Williams story ran second. The brief story, read by anchor Pat Persaud from the set, included sound bites from the condemned killer and the husband of one of the victims.

- KMTV (10 p.m.)—The station led with the Williams execution. The coverage summarized the event, reported Williams' last words, and the reaction of the victims' family members to the execution. Unlike the other stations, KMTV aired a sound bite from Williams' spiritual advisor. It is obvious from the video that the other Omaha television stations recorded the comments; however, KMTV was the only station that aired them at 10 p.m. As can be seen from the following quote, this divergent sound bite did not support the idea that all local TV content is consonant: "I just now witnessed the birth into Heaven of the most good and beautiful man I have ever known. And it was at the hands of the state, an act of violence and just despicability of the state of Nebraska. I am ashamed to be a Nebraskan." The station followed this sound bite with a comparison of the scene outside the prison during the Otey and Joubert executions.

IMPLICATIONS

This case study supported most of the previous assertions about news coverage. In the Otey and Joubert executions, the three stations with 10 o'clock newscasts and special reports portrayed the intense conflict by showing the two sides interacting across a small separation in the penitentiary parking lot. The timing of the Williams execution dramatically altered coverage at 10 p.m., because it took place much earlier in the day. The earlier live coverage reflected the use of the same sources which turned out to be less dramatic and less intense. By emphasizing opponents' silent candlelight vigil, and proponents' signs and "carnival-like atmosphere," the social conflict of the Otey and Joubert executions was portrayed as less complex, more intense, but perhaps not more solvable (Cohen, Adoni, & Bantz, 1990). Interestingly, when events were subdued, as they were in the case of the Williams execution, it was more complex, less intense, and not more solvable. Complexity and intensity seem to be the product of social conditions at the events portrayed.

The three Nebraska executions allow us to see local television news coverage of the death penalty from four perspectives: (a) media organization routines, journalistic beliefs, and source selection as they affected the content; (b) justice as portrayed through a consonant set of social symbols; (c) overwhelming public support for the death penalty in this country has led journalists to avoid tough questioning of public officials; and, (d) the resulting coverage as a social construction of reality that, in turn, may influence future public opinion.

The organizational routines of the Omaha television stations led the Otey and Joubert executions to be major stories that warranted extended live coverage. By the time of the Williams execution, the story had become less important to news organizations for a variety of reasons: the daytime execution, the third in 4 years, the lack of protesters, a killer showing remorse, and the less dramatic portrayal of the crime for Omaha viewers. Nevertheless, organizational routines led all of the stations to cover the three executions in similar ways.

The emphasis on what state officials and demonstrators were saying supports Detweiler's (1987) previous research, which found that journalists believe they should not ignore death penalty demonstrations, even when staged to attract media attention. That emphasis was obvious in the media coverage of the Otey and Joubert executions. In the Williams execution, however, the formula led local television stations to train their cameras on a nearly empty parking lot, searching for demonstrators. In fact, the stations avoided tight close-up camera shots in favor of wide shots. This helped to exaggerate the social distance between the event and viewers, as compared to previous coverage.

There were differences in the way stations covered the three executions. With the Otey execution story, the sound bites from key state officials and others close to the story were emphasized. The Joubert execution was covered less extensively. The Williams execution did not lead in even one newscast, and focused primarily on the two new elements—a daytime execution and that the husband of one of the victims witnessed the electrocution. Beyond this, KMTV aired a sound bite from Williams' spiritual advisor that was openly critical of the state.

The evidence showed that live coverage intensified as the event was occurring at the time of the late night newscast for the three stations with live capability. The decision to broadcast live is an important one, because it elevates the importance of the story. More station personnel and resources are committed to the story. This leads to a larger news hole for the story. With more time to fill, reporters and anchors look to prison demonstrators, government officials, witnesses, relatives of all involved in the case, and legal experts. Selection of sources at the scene is limited by events, and stations opting for live coverage make similar decisions. This is how the "consonant" message of local television news is constructed.

In this case television provided consonance as Elisabeth Noelle-Neumann (1986) described (Carroll et al., 1997). "The question of the likeness of news programs is important, as consonance of reporting tends to restrict selective perception, thus narrowing the formation of public opinion on issues" (Carroll et al., 1997, p. 133). In other words, Omaha television stations provided a uni-form portrayal of the events at the state penitentiary. For the average person in Nebraska, the media coverage of the three executions was the main source of information. These executions were also front-page news for the *Omaha World-Herald* and fodder for local talk radio. As Surette (1992) observed:

> Over time people tend to perceive things the way the media portray them. The media thus play not only a reporting role but a defining role, establishing their au-diences' sense of reality; prescribing society's accepted norms, behaviors, and boundaries; and forwarding the proper means of dealing with injustice. (p. 76)

Local television coverage in the executions portrayed powerful symbols (signs, candlelight vigil, heightened security, prison as a backdrop, etc.), actors (state of-ficials, demonstrators, television anchors, and reporters), and meanings (the le-gitimization of capital punishment, polarizing public debate, etc.). The communication of such meanings is an "essential attribute of culture" (McQuail, 1994, p. 95). In the case of coverage of the Otey and Joubert execu-tions, the negative portrayal of the proponents of the death penalty may have served to promote public cynicism and apathy (Bennett, 1996).

Television coverage of the three executions did not attempt to bridge the gap between proponents and opponents of the death penalty. Even in-studio ex-perts focused on events at the prison scene, rather than the larger social issue of capital punishment. The coverage emphasized the state's role in carrying out the law. As such, the executions of Otey, Joubert, and Williams "solved" the short-term issue, but the long-term social conflict over capital punishment in Nebraska remained. By shifting to a daytime execution and eliminating the party-like atmosphere, the state effectively diminished the power of the chair as a symbol for hundreds of demonstrators rallying outside the prison gates.

What the cameras showed in these three Nebraska executions is a segment of the public that is sharply divided on the capital punishment issue. The supporters and opponents of the death penalty who demonstrated at the penitentiary during the Otey and Joubert executions created a highly unusual event that forced re-porters to evaluate their own news values (Detweiler, 1987; Tunstall, 1971). Such death penalty rallies are viewed as newsworthy, and this allowed the opponents of the death penalty at the prison, through their singing and candlelight vigil, to suc-cessfully portray themselves in the media as more civil than the boisterous propo-nents. KETV anchor Carol Schrader seemed to sense this during the Joubert execution as their cameras panned the large crowd:

> The three Omaha television stations are standing basically in the same perspec-tive you are seeing us. You are seeing the penitentiary behind them. There is an out-of-town station that is parked right in front of the crowd, the proexecution crowd, and the lights they have shining on them and the live shots they are doing are kind of inciting the crowd a little bit. I'm not passing judgment or anything … I'm just saying we make an obvious choice in standing where we do.

Television helps construct a social reality about the death penalty and public attitudes toward it, but the state has the power to manipulate events. Given the nature of source selection, and local television news routines, the dramatic coverage of the three executions may seem unavoidable. Neither the coverage from the prison parking lot, nor analysis by in-studio experts, served to provide viewers with meaningful insight into the capital punishment issue.

It is unfortunate that capital punishment makes news only when there is a heinous crime, during a capital trial, or at the time of execution. It would be better if local television stations could bring themselves to analyze complex social issues outside the heat of an event. Beyond this, lacking a new news angle, coverage of an execution becomes less important to local television stations. Selection of language and graphics can help "normalize" a state execution. Otey was said to be "keeping his appointment" on a "cool, overcast night" in which everyone was "watching the clock." In the Joubert case, the governor was said to be asking people to "keep their cool." And a witness saw "a very polite atmosphere" for the Williams execution. Selection of everyday, routine language ultimately helped distance viewers from an electric chair execution.

Whether the electric chair will continue to be used is not clear, but it is evident that as long as it is in operation, it will be a powerful symbol manipulated by state officials, exploited by demonstrators, propagated by media, and interpreted by the public. Symbols, actors, and meanings in local television coverage are of the utmost importance in understanding public interest in the social construction of capital punishment. In the next chapter, we turn our attention to the issue of the gender or race of a suspect, convict, or victim in local television news coverage.

CHAPTER SUMMARY

This chapter focused on how local television news covers executions. The death penalty was examined as a social construction of reality. A high degree of consonance was found between competing stations' coverage. Local television news tended to follow the lead of official state sources. The future of local television news coverage of death penalty cases depends, in part, on how state officials approach future executions, what methods of capital punishment are used, and how the public reacts to media coverage. Local television newsrooms will continue to view heinous crimes as newsworthy, and they will be faced with important decisions about how to cover punishment.

DISCUSSION QUESTIONS

1. How did the four stations cover each event? To what extent did they use routine sources? How similar was their coverage?

2. How did each of the stations portray the intense social conflict between proponents and opponents of the death penalty?
3. To what extent were constructions of social conflict portrayed as less complex, more intense, and more solvable than they really are?
4. If coverage legitimizes the state action of capital punishment, how does that happen? What role will media coverage play in future executions as well as the evolution of capital punishment in the country?
5. How does the consonant local television view of executions fit with print and radio coverage? How might the Internet affect future coverage?

8

Minorities and Crime News

"Television news relies on visual imagery for storytelling, even if the images may contribute to the kinds of stereotypical beliefs that advance racism and discrimination."

—Christopher P. Campbell, communication professor (1995, p. 71)

Local TV news coverage of crime inevitably raises issues of race. The portrayal of African American and Hispanic suspects may create an impression with White viewers that reinforce stereotypes. Likewise, the race of victims may also be important. Local television news personalizes coverage by focusing on people and their emotions, including fear. Conflict is a driving force in news judgment, and racial conflict may be seen as a dramatic story.

The issue of media coverage of race has received renewed attention in the wake of former network television producer Av Westin's charge that "bias" remains a problem:

> It's safe to say that in almost all newsrooms, blatant bigotry and intolerance do not exist. What does exist, however, are preconceived notions about race and ethnicity that can shape story selection and content. The conventional wisdom among many assignment editors is that white viewers will tune out if blacks and Latinos are featured in segments. That view can influence the choice of the person who will provide the "expert" sound bite. There is no question that a lack of racial sensitivity affects news judgment. It is a problem that goes to the heart of fair and balanced presentation of the news on television. (Westin, 2000, p. 21)

Westin (2000) provided only anecdotal evidence from interviews with newsroom employees. He claimed that the television news business uses code words, such as "It's not good television," to exclude minority experts from newscasts. One employee told Westin the following: "My bosses have essentially made it clear: 'We do not feature black people.' Period. I mean, it's said. Actually, they whisper it, 'Is she white?'" (p. 21). No data are available that would suggest how pervasive this bias might be in local television news. Westin confronted the question of racism in local television news crime coverage:

> In Freedom Forum roundtables around the country, the public raised concerns that African Americans were more typically shown being arrested as suspects than other minorities or whites. In some newsrooms, producers have adopted proactive procedures to make as certain as possible that blacks are not automatically seen as the villains in crime reporting. (p. 23)

There is no national study of local television news that reports on the degree of racism in crime coverage, or the attempts by local stations to react to the criticism. Critical theories about race, however, are important in understanding the portrayal of minorities. For more than a decade, researchers have been studying the media treatment of minorities.

THE PORTRAYAL OF AFRICAN AMERICANS

In American mass media, African Americans have been portrayed stereotypically. The Missouri School of Journalism (2000, p. 133) outlined four criticisms of news coverage of minorities:

- Stories do not show minorities in context. Most stories picture minorities as criminals or victims or emphasize conflict.
- There is too much focus on atypical behavior, both good and bad, on crisis, or, on the other hand, of "colorful" festivals, holidays and other "exotic" aspects of nonmajority life.
- There is too much focus on entertainment figures and on minorities who are "firsts" in their disciplines.
- There is not enough coverage showing minority people participating in the day-to-day life of their communities.

On the negative side, there is the stereotype of African Americans as "dangerous criminals" (Oliver, 1999, p. 46). On the positive side, there may be the stereotype of African Americans as successful entertainers and athletes (Campbell, 1995). In one experiment conducted to test White viewers' memory of a criminal suspect in a television newscast, participants who had seen a White suspect in the news story were more likely to mistakenly identify him as an African American (Oliver, 1999). "One implication of the results of this study is that viewers' memories of racial and crime-related information in the news may serve to sustain racial stereotyping, even under conditions where African Americans and Caucasians are portrayed in similar ways" (Oliver, 1999, p. 56).

In a content analysis of Los Angeles and Orange County local television news in 1995 and 1996, Dixon and Linz (2000) found that "Blacks and Latinos are significantly more likely than Whites to be portrayed as lawbreakers on tele-vision news" (p. 131). They also found the following:

- Whites were significantly more likely to be portrayed as law defenders than lawbreakers.
- There was an over representation in the portrayal of African Americans as lawbreakers compared to California crime statistics, whereas Latinos and Whites were under represented.
- Compared to county employment records, there was an over representa-tion of White police officers, an under representation of Latino police of-ficers, and an accurate representation of African American police officers portrayed in local TV news.

The findings suggest that the over representation of African Americans as law-breakers continues to be a problem: "We suggest that the immediate work must be undertaken with regard to how these portrayals might encourage or discour-age stereotyping and increase fear of African Americans" (Dixon & Linz, 2000,

---

In 1992, local and national TV news crews were faced with coverage of riots in Los Angeles. Analyses of news coverage have found that it focused on African Ameri-cans as rioters and Korean business people and Whites as victims. The roles of La-tinos were downplayed despite the fact that they made up more than half of rioters arrested and one third of store owners. Although network coverage seemed to be issue-oriented, local TV news focused on specific incidents of neighborhood vio-lence and movement toward restoring "law and order." It has been argued that such coverage reinforces racial stereotypes.

"Studies of television news portrayals of African Americans indicate that tele-vision seems to prefer the coverage and discussion of crime" (Martindale & Dunlap, 1997, p. 128). One year-long study of large market TV news found two significant distortions:

- Crime is violent although statistics show that much urban crime is nonviolent.
- Criminals are Black although statistics show that Whites account for over half of the arrests for violent crime.

Viewers are primed to see crime through the coverage as reinforcing their ra-cial stereotypes. Crime is often presented as a black-and-white issue in coverage, and stereotyping today is seen as more subtle than previously portrayed.

Source: Martindale, C., & Dunlap, L. R. (1997). The African Americans. In B. A. D. Keever, C. Martindale, & M. A. Weston (Eds.), *U.S. news coverage of racial minorities* (pp. 122–130). Westport, CT:

BOX 8.1   Broadcast Coverage of Urban Strife.

p. 151). However, another study in 1993 and 1994 of one station in that market found that non-Whites "were not substantially over represented" in violent crime news coverage (Gilliam et al., 1996, p. 10).

In a previous study, African American respondents were shown publicity photographs of 12 local TV news reporters in Pittsburgh, PA—African American and White men and women. The study found that an overwhelming majority of respondents viewed African American newscasters as more attractive and more believable, but less than half of the respondents found those same African American newscasters as better performers than Whites (Johnson, 1984). The highest rankings for African American newscasters came from younger and more educated African American respondents.

Local television stations that hire Black reporters and anchors may be viewed as promoting a positive role model (Entman, 1994b; Campbell, 1995). Sports is a type of reporting that emphasizes use of African Americans in coverage: "Clearly, this a reflection of White America's acceptance—which was initially reluctant, at best—of Black athletic success; it also reflects the fact that sports is one area in which African Americans have been allowed to compete on an even field" (Campbell, 1995, p. 63). Although sports coverage has promoted positive images through superstars such as Michael Jordan, Shaquille O'Neal, Tiger Woods, Ken Griffey, Jr., and Serena and Venus Williams, news coverage continues to be criticized for its disproportionately framing crime stories involving African American suspects. Gandy (1994) wondered aloud whether the hiring of minority newsroom staffers would alter the framing of stories by reducing negative stereotypes: "The best framing is one that produces relative equality or balance between types across similar stories" (p. 48).

Local news coverage, where individuals obtain much of their information about crime, feed a complex social environment: "the stereotyping of African Americans and crime has a long history and is a reflection of many variables" (Oliver, 1999, p. 47). Local television news media may participate through their portrayals in what has been termed a form of "modern racism" (Entman, 1994b, p. 33). Beyond this:

> This form of racism has three basic characteristics: first, a general animosity among whites toward African Americans; second, a resistance to black political demands—for instance, affirmative action or hiring quotas; and third, a belief that racial discrimination is a thing of the past. Entman found the portrayal of crime on local television news to contribute to the first characteristic; that is, the menacing images of African American criminals contribute to a modern racist hostility toward African Americans. (Campbell, 1995, p. 89)

Entman's (1992) limited study of local television news found that "crime reporting made Blacks look particularly threatening" (1992, p. 342). A content analysis of the evening news on four Chicago television stations in 1989 and 1990 found evidence of indirect racism: "… that depict Blacks, in crime, as more physically threatening and, in politics, as more demanding than comparable White activists or leaders" (Entman, 1992, p. 341). Entman contended that the problem of racism is masked by the hiring of black reporters and anchors: "The mix of these two views of blacks encourages modern white racism—hostility, rejection and denial toward black aspirations" (p. 341). The portrayal of African Americans in network news also appeared to be stereotypical in that these images involved a narrow range of roles (Entman, 1994a). More generally, crime is perceived by the public as one of the most important problems facing the country, and news coverage that portrays black criminals feeds modern racist stereotypes: "Not only does news coverage highlight violent crime, it also links the issues of face and crime by over representing minorities in the role of violent criminals and by according them distinctive forms of coverage" (Gilliam, Jr., Iyengar, Simon, & Wright, 1996, p. 7). Coverage of minorities may be seen as a "parable of poor and minority violent offenders" in society: "On a personal level, the ways we choose to distinguish ourselves from others can serve as a basis for fear, hatred, and even violence" (Brownstein, 2000, p. 133). It is argued that race and class matter in the United States:

> They matter not only in the degree to which individuals are likely to be violent offenders or are liable to be its victims, but also in terms of how we view violence and the people who behave in violent ways. In fact, race and class even matter in terms of whether we are likely to believe that a person could have been the perpetrator or even the victim of violence. (Brownstein, 2000, p. 134)

Brownstein (2000) reported that in 1995 there were more than 600,000 arrests for violent crime, and 54% were White. "Still, Americans have been and remain quick to think of people of color as violent and to think of violent offenders as black" (p. 139). In the most recent available data in 1997 from the United States Department of Justice, the number of arrests for violent crime dropped to 500,621. At the same time, the percentage of Whites arrested increased to 56.8% (*Sourcebook of Criminal Justice Statistics*, 1998, pp. 342–344). It has been argued that although African Americans make up about 14% of the population in the United States, they represented more than 40% of arrests for violent crimes, and this may help drive the stereotype.

The emphasis of violent crime coverage in local television news means that the stereotype is imprinted on viewers' minds through the daily deluge of images. As has been stated earlier, local TV news crime coverage typically identifies suspects by race: "The police sketches, like the mug shots routinely appear on local television newscasts' crime stories, carry connotative messages of wrongdoing, of danger, of conviction-before-trial" (Campbell, 1995, p. 71). Likewise, surveillance camera video (such as that recorded in a convenience store armed robbery) typically shows race. The existence of video, of course, increases the value of the story to the local television newsroom. To some extent, news people should not be faulted for use of interesting video, given that television is a visual medium. However, "... when preoccupation with visual effects overrides news judgment, it encourages emphasis on action rather than on significance and the playing up of the trivial or exciting occurrences simply because they can be covered by cameras" (MacNeil, 1968, p. 35, as quoted in Campbell, 1995, p. 75).

RACE AND LOCAL TV NEWS

In a year-long study of one Los Angeles television station, the local news averaged three crime stories per day, and crime stories led half of the broadcasts:

> ... although blacks commit violent and nonviolent crime at about the same rate, the media coverage of black crime is distinctly more violent than nonviolent.... Conversely, media coverage of white crime is distinctly more nonviolent than violent ... even though whites are only slightly less likely ... to engage in violent rather than nonviolent crime. (Gilliam et al., 1996, p. 13)

Heider's (2000) study suggested that minorities in Albuquerque, NM, and Honolulu, HI, believed that they were covered by local television newsrooms only during ethnic festivals or in the context of crime coverage:

> When news makers continually choose to include images of people of color as perpetrators of crimes and omit images of people of color as normal citizens, they reinforce the idea that people of color primarily exist outside the bounds of legitimate social behavior.... In discerning what stories will be covered and how crime stories will be presented, news organizations send out messages about where crime occurs, and what crime is routine and what crime is out of the ordinary. (p. 42)

Heider contended that the nightly mention of murders and robberies in specific parts of town leads the audience to see those locations as unsafe. Thus, the reinforcement of stereotypical assumptions about race may be driven by local TV news coverage: "... crime coverage may be reinforcing hegemony by reinforcing inscribed ideas about who commits crime (people of color), where most crimes occur (communities of color), and where crimes should not occur (White, affluent neighborhoods)" (p. 43).

Even when news coverage focuses on a White suspect, White viewers may misidentify the suspect months later as an African American: "This finding is consistent with the idea that stereotypes are maintained not only by attending to and remembering information that is consistent, but also by discounting information that is inconsistent" (Oliver, 1999, p. 56).

In other words, White viewers who associate crime with minorities because of racist beliefs will misperceive news to remain consistent. "In its proclivity for coverage of urban crime, local television journalism compounds stereotypical notions about African American life" (Campbell, 1995, p. 72). In America's large cities, where crime is a part of everyday life, local television newsrooms often are led by White managers. Often, African American reporters and anchors are found in limited numbers. According to media researcher Vernon Stone, minorities made up about 18% of the overall television news workforce, and among news directors minorities made up about 8%. Stone wrote "The white ceiling remains" (Stone, 2001).

The Board of Directors of the RTNDA, in June, 2000, called for newsrooms to be more "proactive" in efforts to "hire, train and promote people of color into management roles." RTNDA research estimated that 21% of newsroom personnel and 14% of local news directors are minorities. "Newsrooms need to reflect the communities they serve," said RTNDA Chairman Robert Garcia. The resolution read as follows:

> The Radio–Television News Directors Association believes that diversity must be a top priority in the nation's electronic newsrooms.
>
> Toward that goal, we urge our membership, and electronic media ownership, to make a commitment to recruit, hire, develop and retain top managers and executives who reflect the diverse makeup of the communities we serve.
>
> RTNDA is committed to diversity, and stands ready with resources and services to assist news organizations. (RTNDA, 15 June 2000)

Garcia added the following: "This resolution tells the industry that we are serious about our diversity efforts, and that we want minorities hired, trained and ultimately promoted into management ranks." < http://www.rtnda.org/news/2000/abcfmminm.shtml>

The domination of newsroom decision making by White managers may lead to content that promotes the stereotypical view that all minorities belong in a single category, and this does not promote understanding between the races (Gandy & Baron, 1998). As a matter of "cocultural communication," minorities may be seen as "muted groups" because of the following:

> Those groups that function at the top of the social hierarchy determine to a great extent the communication system of the entire society. Over time, the structures of this system—which reflect the world view of the dominant group members—are reinforced as the appropriate communicative system for both dominant and non-dominant group members. (Orbe, 1998, pp. 233–234)

Local television news would be considered part of the larger communication system that reflects a White majority view. The traditional Eurocentric world view has been challenged by the research community (Delgado, 1998). For example, minority group members, like other ethnic and racial group members, are not all alike; they vary demographically (Delgado, 1998; Orbe, 1995). Me-

TABLE 8.1

Overrepresentation of Minorities of Victims

Racial and Ethnic Groups	Population Age 12 or older	Victims of Serious Violence	Rates per 1,000
Total	100	100	20
White	77	65	17
Black	12	20	34
Other	3	4	24
Hispanic	8	12	29

Note. Blacks and to a lesser degree Hispanics were overrepresented among victims, relative to their proportions of the general population age 12 or older. Whites, Blacks, and others exclude Hispanics.

Source: Craig A. Perkins, "Age Patterns of Victims of Serious Violent Crime," United States Department of Justice, Special Report, July 1997.

dia are seen as stereotyping disenfranchised groups, such as African American men (Orbe, 1998). However, "African Americans are regarded as an ethnic culture, one which is distinguished by a shared historical orientation as well as a prevailing group identity" (Orbe, 1995, p. 61). African Americans, as a group, have been said to identify with (a) "soul" that "emphasizes the historical African American culture and affirms the importance of acceptance and perseverance;" and (b) "black nationalism" that "values African American culture and emphasizes revolution against racism, colonialism, and imperialism" (del Carmen, 2000, p. 137). The challenge for local television journalists is to recognize and understand that culture, and also be open to treating African Americans as unique individuals. The emphasis on Black suspects in crime coverage tends to reinforce stereotypes for White viewers:

> Blacks often are identified in these reports, particularly in arrest scenes on local television, as "perps" (police shorthand for "perpetrators"); but it's not always explained that statistics show most "black crime" to be committed not against whites but against other blacks in the black ghettoes common to major American cities.... It may be, therefore, that the public fears crime not so much as a personal threat but more as a destructive social force—and, worse that the heavy and unfair burden a get-tough imprisonment policy imposes on the black community also as seen as from a distance—as if it were happening elsewhere, of no personal concern to unaffected whites. (Westfeldt & Wicker, 1998, p. 51)

Local television news is often limited in crime coverage by the availability of visuals other than "mug shots," and these may feed racial stereotypes. Still, newsrooms must be careful to portray crime in all parts of a city on an equal basis. Beyond this, racial stereotypes of viewers might be challenged by everyday coverage of African American men and women as routine sources in news stories.

VICTIMS OF CRIME

Victims and others, such as witnesses, are used in the news production process, but remain outside of it:

> A crime victim who can supply good, newsworthy emotion results in a story's becoming higher level and influences when victims are contacted, how they are contacted, the types of questions that are asked, and what is presented about the victim. (Chermak, 1995, p. 85)

Blacks and Hispanics, according to U.S. Department of Justice statistics, across all age groups, were more at risk from violence than Whites—1 in 30 Blacks, 1 in 35 Hispanics, and 1 in 58 Whites in the 1990s.

As has been suggested previously, sometimes stories in which Black suspects are charged with crimes against White victims are sensationalized by local television news:

> Crime victims are influential in determining why certain crime stories are selected, how stories are produced, which stories are presented, and which crimes get filtered out of the process. Whether a crime is selected and whether it is promoted to a secondary, a primary, or even a super primary level can be influenced by the status of the victim. (Chermak, 1995, p. 62)

Chermak added that crime victims provide human interest to a story through their emotional reactions.

Typically, death or extreme physical harm qualifies a story as newsworthy, but Chermak (1995) suggested that the existence of video creates a unique circumstance, "raising the newsworthiness of assaults and aggravated assaults as television crime stories" (p. 132). In such cases, racial stereotypes might be called into question by the majority of viewers. For example, when White Los Angeles police officers were videotaped beating motorist Rodney King following a traffic stop, and that home video made it into the hands of local television news reports, the audience reacted to the unfairness portrayed on the tape. The event raised awareness and public concern about police brutality, and it triggered more intense media coverage of the issue (Rogers & Dearing, 1988, in Graber, 2000, p. 73). Local TV news coverage of individual events may have a cumulative effect on public perceptions about the crime issue.

Entman (1994b) observed that "... newsroom procedures and definitions of news combine with selected aspects of the real world to encourage negative stereotypes about blacks" (p. 31). Entman's research found that local television newsrooms treated Black and White criminal defendants differently. Blacks were more often shown in mugshots without being named, were more likely shown in police custody, and were less likely in positive law enforcement roles: "The overall image of crime and violence from local news is one in which minorities, especially blacks, play a heavy role in causing violence but contribute disproportionately little toward helping society cope with it" (p. 32). It is not much of a leap, then, to suggest that the day-to-day coverage of crime news in this way may influence public opinion on the importance of the crime issue and what needs to be done about it. Heider (2000) suggested two remedies to the problem: (a) more reporters in the field covering community issues, and (b) education of viewers and news people. Local TV news faces increasing competition from new technologies, and Heider contended that to survive a station must "... convince viewers that it is in touch with the local community" (p. 95). Coverage of minorities will become increasingly important as the racial composition of each local television market becomes more diverse. In fact, minorities and women appear to be more visible on television news than ever (Newkirk, 2000). Nevertheless, the view of white America that equality has been achieved is tempered by cultural concerns: "African Americans and their minority counterparts are still woefully under represented in the industry and are far from integrated into the newsroom culture" (Newkirk, 2000, p. 194). Therefore, it is likely that criticisms about how local television newsrooms cover minorities will continue.

CHAPTER SUMMARY

This chapter discussed the importance of race in local television news crime coverage. The race of those arrested, as well as those victimized, often is an issue because visual images are a crucial part of any story.

DISCUSSION QUESTIONS

1. If you were a late evening television news producer, how would you deal with a story about an armed robbery at a convenience store, if there was no video? Would it matter that there was no injuries? Would the race of the suspect be part of the story? Why or why not? Would it make a difference if the store were located in an inner-city neighborhood or a suburb?
2. Do you agree or disagree that local television news coverage contributes to promoting racial stereotypes? Why or why not? What other social factors besides television news may reinforce stereotypical beliefs?
3. Should race of a victim in a crime story ever make a difference in local television news coverage? Why or why not?
4. How does the daily coverage of a particular crime event such as a murder, a drug bust, or a school shooting translate into coverage of larger issues of crime in our society?
5. How might the findings in past research concerning portrayal of minorities in local television news have a long-term influence on public policy?

9

Crime News and the Elderly

"I think they [news media] are denying the fact that the demographics are there and they cannot quite accept them, yet."

—Myrna Lewis, sociologist (Cable News Network, 1993)

Older adults watch television news. Professional and academic research repeatedly show that the elderly segment of our population is the one age group broadcasters may rely on for viewing local news. This chapter examines the impact of the elderly as viewers and participants in local television crime coverage. To understand the importance of this issue, the impact of aging in America must be addressed.

GERONTOLOGY AND AN AGING POPULATION

The older population in the United States is increasing dramatically, and it has been referred to as the "graying of America" (Barrow, 1996, p. 6). Americans are living longer due to a healthier lifestyle that includes a better diet and medical care (Reinhardt, 2000). Census projections show that by the year 2040, the nation could have more people over age 65 than under age 21, and more than one in four Americans will be 65 or older (Usdansky, 1992). In the 1990 census figures, adults 65 and over accounted for one out of eight Americans, compared to 1 in 25 at the beginning of the 20th century. Furthermore, the over-85 age group represents the fastest-growing segment of the population (Dychtwald & Flower, 1989).

Scholarly interest in the area of mass media and older adults continues to increase (Roy & Harwood, 1997), however, television news executives have been slow to consider this growing segment of the audience (Hilt, 1992). Broadcasters, either through a conscious decision or an involuntary act, follow the desires of society put forth in the social gerontology disengagement theory. The theory is a useful framework for the examination of attitudes about older people.

The disengagement theory (Cumming & Henry, 1961; Passuth & Bengtson, 1988; Young, 1979) argues that society and the elderly are mutually obliged to withdraw from each other. The authors of this theory, Elaine Cumming and William Henry, maintained that the process is functional to both society and the individual; it enables society to make room for more efficient young people while allowing the elderly time to prepare for their eventual total withdrawal from social life—death. Cumming and Henry argued that the disengagement theory should actually be considered an interpersonal communication theory because mass communication researchers say television serves as a substitute for interpersonal contacts among elderly people: "In television, especially, the image which is presented makes available nuances of appearance and gesture to which ordinary social perception is attentive and to which interaction is cued" (Horton & Wohl, 1986, p. 185).

The theory of disengagement has generated much criticism. Barrow (1996) contended that one might just as well speak of society excluding the elderly as disengaging them; perhaps the withdrawal of older people is a reaction to a society that excludes them. It may be that older adults are being pushed out of society, and television contributes to the disengagement by not showing or speaking about elderly people in its programs. Thorson (1995) wrote that the disengagement theory, like many studies of the aged, tended to lump all older adults into one group and not allow for individual differences. Whitmore (1995) concluded that there is little knowledge about the portrayal of older people by the news media, and that television news tends to treat the elderly in a superficial manner by focusing on the extreme.

Ryff, Marshall, and Clarke (1999) maintained that the disengagement theory has strong microlevel conceptualizations of social structure. Social construction of reality may also enter into a process because the "individual and society" are engaged in an ongoing relationship (p. 18). Ryff et al. declared that reality feeds back on the individual, and is embodied in written and other institutional forms. One type of institutional form is television.

THE VIEWING HABITS OF OLDER AMERICANS

Elderly people spend more time with television than any other medium (Louis Harris, 1975; Moss & Lawton, 1982; Nussbaum, Thompson, & Robinson, 1989) and watch more TV than younger people (Bower, 1973). Older adults spend far more time watching television than reading newspapers, and watch more television than any other age group (Atkins, Jenkins, & Perkins, 1991; Moss & Lawton, 1982). While watching television, the older viewer prefers news, documentaries, and public affairs (Bower, 1973; Davis, 1971; Davis, Edwards, Bartel, & Martin, 1976; Davis & Westbrook, 1985; Goodman, 1990; Korzenny & Neuendorf, 1980; Rubin & Rubin, 1982a; Rubin & Rubin, 1982b; Scales, 1996; Steiner, 1963; Wenner, 1976). Older viewers are major consumers of television news, preferring television news over other media (Doolittle, 1979) because they view it as a way to become aware of current events rather than as a diversion (Davis & Davis, 1985). Frequency of television use and total viewing time increases with age up to about 69 years, before showing a slight decline (Louis Harris, 1975). People 55 years and over watch an average of 7 more hr of television per week than younger adults (Nielsen, 1975). Nielsen found elderly people watch between 30 and 35 hr of TV per week.

Bower's study (1973) found that "older persons spend more of their time watching the news." His 55-year-and-over group had the highest rate of any age group for viewing news, information and public affairs. Steiner (1963) had reported similar findings. Steiner found people 55 to 64-years-old watched 16.4 television news and information programs per week, and those 65 years and older watched 22.4 programs per week. These were the two largest age groups for viewing television news and information programming.

Doolittle (1979) separated an older cohort into three subgroups: younger seniors (48 to 66 years); old seniors (67 to 74 years); and older seniors (75 to 93 years). Of the three subgroups, television news usage was the highest for old seniors (67 to 74 years). Overall, these respondents rated television as most credible.

In a study conducted by Kent and Rush (1976), 99% of the elderly persons surveyed said they watched television news. This heavy use of television news remained 14 years later, when Goodman (1990) found that older men and women favored television for their national news and information, but preferred newspapers for local news.

Research conducted for the ABC Television Network found that viewers age 50 and older were significantly more interested in news than younger generations (Wurtzel, 1992). Thanks to health care improvements, people in their 60s and older are living longer, and have more disposable income than ever before (Lieberman & McCray, 1994). Americans 50 years of age and older control half of this country's discretionary income and 77% of its assets (Grey Advertising, 1988), and the 65 to 74 cohort has the highest percentage of discretionary income of any 10-year cohort (Wolfe, 1987). Lieberman and McCray (1994) maintained that news and information needed to be relevant to all groups, if the media wanted to keep its audiences. They found that 90% of people at retirement age or over said keeping up with the news is extremely important.

While all of this is happening, news has become a major profit center at local stations (Wicks, 1989). However, broadcast news, entertainment, and advertising have been geared toward younger adults, the so-called money makers who buy goods. Over the years the television networks have cancelled programs which attracted an older viewing audience, such as *Red Skelton* and *Lawrence Welk*. Later, NBC targeted older viewers in the 1980s with series such as *Golden*

Girls, but "cancelled those programs in an effort to attract a younger audience" (Head, Sterling, & Schofield, 1994, p. 308). By the end of the 1990s, American broadcast television networks had remained centered on attracting a younger audience, and the only programming targeting older adults was relatively inexpensive news magazines. Some cable networks such as MSNBC, CNBC, CNN, Fox News Channel, C–SPAN, and HGTV had older audiences during some times of day.

Numerous studies show that use of the media increases during middle age through the retirement years (Dimmick, McCain, & Bolton, 1979). Almost 40 years ago Glick and Levy (1962) referred to the elderly as "embracers" of television; they seem to have a "close identification with television, a rather undiscriminating and accepting attitude toward it, and usually, [make] great use of the medium" (p. 55, p. 44).

Several explanations have been given for age-related trends in media use. Comstock, Chaffee, Katzman, McCombs, and Roberts (1978) grouped the elderly along with the poor and ethnic minorities into the category of "disadvantaged." They said this group depends on television more than any other news medium for knowledge and information. The elderly audience's use of the broadcast medium may be related to the ease with which it can be received. Television, beyond the cost of the set, costs less than newspapers and magazines. In addition, failing eyesight can make reading difficult or impossible (Chaffee & Wilson, 1975).

Another reason given for increased use of the media by elderly people is that television and newspapers have become substitutes for interpersonal contacts (Davis, 1971; Graney, 1975; Graney & Graney, 1974; Rubin & Rubin, 1982b). Because of loneliness and disengagement, older adults turn to mass media for their information about the outside world (Atkin, 1976; Hess, 1974; Powell & Williamson, 1985; Schramm, 1969). In fact, older viewers may participate in para-social interaction—a process in which a viewer comes to see a television personality as an important person in their life (Horton & Wohl, 1986).

As discussed earlier, the disengagement theory of aging suggests that as people grow older they are likely to show less interest in society's problems (Cassata, 1985). Cassata found that television news allows them to feel connected to the world, and the news also supplies them with the information required for "adaptive functioning." This finding has been offered as evidence to challenge the disengagement hypothesis. People disengaged from society would not seem likely to be interested in television news, but elderly people show high interest. Atkin (1976) suggested that the preference for news and information in television viewing is a direct attempt to compensate for the stable and unexciting world of older adults. Schramm (1969) interpreted this as their way of keeping up with society rather than a means of disengagement. He wrote that older people use television to keep in touch, combat progressive disengagement, and maintain a sense of belonging to society. Lowenthal and Boler (1965) found those aged adults who voluntarily disengaged from their social activities decreased use of media, and those involuntarily disengaged increased their use. Kubey (1981) found that television may help substitute for the interpersonal information network that existed when the individual went out into the community to work. The increased leisure time that accompanies retirement may account for some of the higher consumption rates of television news by elderly people. The substitution theory has been offered as an alternative to the disengagement theory. The substitution theory of aging holds that older persons will tend to substitute mass media communication for interpersonal communication when the latter is unavailable, or extremely difficult to accomplish (Bliese, 1986).

TELEVISION PORTRAYAL OF OLDER AMERICANS

Considerable research has been conducted in two theoretical fields relative to the portrayal of elderly people in the mass media and specifically on television. Two primary hypotheses about media effects have emerged from this research.

First, the cultivation theory holds that people watching television acquire a view of the real world shaped by the televised content they view. Gerbner (1969) noted that, if elderly people are portrayed on television as incompetent, viewers may begin to think that is true. Signorielli & Gerbner's (1978) prime-time television analysis of more than 9,000 TV characters found that elderly people were not often represented. When they were, they often had problems and were reliant on younger people for help (Northcott, 1975); were more likely to be villains than heroes (Aronoff, 1974); or, simply were portrayed in a negative light (Davis & Kubey, 1982). More recent research (Bell, 1992) found that negative stereotypes of elderly people in prime-time television have been replaced by more positive stereotypes. However, Bell added that these portrayals should mirror the demographics of the country, not just in the number of older people shown on television, but also in gender, race, class, marital and health status. Gerbner (1993) found in a study of women and minorities on television that older people are greatly under represented, and seem to be declining instead of increasing as in real life. Cultivation theorists would say that heavy television viewers may think that few people are elderly and that elderly persons were of less consequence because they were rarely seen on television.

Atchley (1991) wrote that it is difficult to generalize about the way aging is portrayed on television, because it is such a varied and complex medium. He found little research had been conducted into the portrayal of older adults in television news. Other research in the area of television's portrayal of elderly people includes Saturday morning cartoons (Bishop & Krause, 1984; Levinson, 1973; Powers, 1992), game shows (Danowski, 1975), television commercials (Francher, 1973; Hiemstra, Goodman, Middlemiss, Vosco, & Ziegler, 1983; Schreiber & Boyd, 1980; Swayne & Greco, 1987), fictional television (Greenberg, Korzenny, & Atkin, 1979), prime-time television (Cassata & Irwin, 1989; Dail, 1988; Petersen, 1973) and soap operas (Barton, 1977;

Cassata, Anderson, & Skill, 1980; Cassata, Anderson, & Skill, 1983; Downing, 1974; Elliott, 1984; Ramsdell, 1973).

A second hypothesis about media effects involves agenda setting, which suggests the media will influence the way people think by focusing viewers' attention on specific issues (Nussbaum et al., 1989). The media set the agenda for the audience by emphasizing certain topics and by slighting other issues through omission. Agenda setting could enter television news programs through event bias. Television newscasts tend to report events such as fires and accidents rather than nonevent issues such as the plight of elderly people. Television may reinforce stereotypical attitudes toward elderly people (Gerbner, Gross, Signorielli, & Morgan, 1980). Lonely elderly viewers in one study showed greater interest in viewing negative rather than positive portrayals, whereas nonlonely viewers exhibited the opposite preference (Mares & Cantor, 1992). Results of a national survey published in *Parade* magazine (Clements, 1993) showed that more than half of the respondents feel the elderly are portrayed favorably in television (62%), movies (59%), and advertising (55%). One respondent who disagreed said that the average person who does not have close contact with the elderly and only sees them through the media would get an incorrect perspective. "This may be one reason why many people treat the elderly as children, as if someone else would be better at deciding what's best for them" (Clements, 1993, p. 5).

Many Americans fear growing old. Friedan (1993) placed much of the blame for this fear of aging with the media. Studies of television's portrayal of elderly people rarely conclude that the portrayals are positive. Also, although many older persons spend substantial time with TV and like to watch it, such older viewers have not been a significant factor in commercial television programming decisions (Carmichael, 1976; Carmichael, Botan, & Hawkins, 1988). Programming decisions are often based on the number of people watching a particular show—the ratings. If the ratings are low, or if the advertisers do not buy commercial time because they do not want to market their product to the type of people who watch that program, the show soon will be off the air. The ABC television network, along with the other major television networks (CBS, NBC, and FOX), considers its core viewers to be adults in the 18- to 49-year-old age group, teenagers, and children ages 2 to 11 (Wurtzel, 1992). According to Rubin (1988), programmers and advertisers typically have ignored the needs and wishes of over 20% of the population, those past the age of 54. In fact, television advertisers control what is seen. Elderly persons do not feel television commercials give an accurate picture of older people (Louis Harris, 1981). Research has found a positive relation between television orientation and concern for one's personal and financial well-being (Rahtz, Sirgy, & Meadow, 1989). This might be useful in helping advertisers select the appeal which would be most effective among elderly people. Network television has all but turned its back on viewers older than 50, and the graying of America is not accurately reflected in prime-time television (Kogan, 1992). Kogan's article concludes by

posing the question of whether it is television's job to serve viewers or advertisers. "I don't think you want to hear the answer to that question," one ABC executive responded. Prime-time entertainment programming is an important
lead-in for local television news departments' late evening newscasts. Industry
research has shown that highly rated entertainment programs boost the ratings
of the local news that follows.

THE ATTITUDES OF BROADCASTERS

A consistent theme in gerontological literature is that negative attitudes toward
aging influence how a person cares for or perceives the elderly (Powell, Thorson,
Kara, & Uhl, 1990). The types of news stories or newscasts that air on a television
station are influenced by the broadcast managers. Therefore, those managers' attitudes toward the elderly could influence those stories or programs.

There have been calls for research into the needs of media personnel for information about the aged (Atkin, 1976). Barton and Schreiber (1978) called for
an examination of the internal structures and functions of media organizations
as they relate to aging. Such research would reveal how aging as a content topic
and as a social issue among staff members is dealt with at critical stages of the
mass communication process. More than 10 years ago Rubin (1982) listed six
areas of inquiry for future research into television and aging: a) continue examination and development of functional life-position indicators as alternatives to
chronological age, b) continue examination of the interactive communication
needs and media uses of aging and aged persons and how certain media behaviors gratify these needs, c) research the area of nontelevision media and aging,
d) provide empirical evidence to establish the extent of television's social influence, e) examine the uses which older people can make of the evolving new
technologies and the impact of these technologies on television programming
and other media content, and f) examine the policies and procedures of television in monitoring their presentations of aging-related issues and portrayals.

Research into network television news divisions found that the organizational structure was the most important factor in the framing, selection, and
production of news (Epstein, 1973). Epstein (1973) concluded that much of
how news was gathered, processed, and delivered at the network level was related to organizational needs and constraints. Gans (1979) found that journalists, whether in broadcasting or print, share messages about society with their
audience. Goedkoop (1988) found the same could be said for journalists at the
local television level.

The general manager is the person in charge of the local television station—either through ownership of the station or by appointment from the station's board of directors. The general manager is the person who would hire the
news director. The news director is the key individual in any local news operation (Goedkoop, 1988). In most newsrooms, the news director is responsible for

managerial duties such as hiring and firing, purchasing equipment and budget-ing, and setting newsroom policy. The news director is ultimately responsible for the news coverage (Fang, 1985). There is a growing managerial role on the part of news directors that is related to the increasing role of the news department in the finances and programming of television stations (Quarderer & Stone, 1989a; Quarderer & Stone, 1989b; Stone, 1988). However, because local news can take several hours of airtime per day, major decisions involving the news-casts are made in concert between the general manager and news director, and possibly managers from other station departments.

The news director would hire the assignment editor—the person in charge of the day-to-day coverage of news. This person selects and assigns the stories to be covered by the newsroom employees on a given day. These decisions are based on the events of the day, such as government meetings and crime reports, and policies established by station management. The news director would also hire the newscast producer. Producers decide which stories run in a newscast, and the order of the stories within a newscast.

Although general managers and news directors set the policy for news cover-age, assignment editors and producers carry out that policy on a day-to-day ba-sis. As a group, these four players ultimately have strong influence on what viewers see in their nightly local television newscasts (Hilt & Lipschultz, 1996; Hilt & Lipschultz, 1999). To paraphrase Herbert Gans (1979), assignment edi-tors and producers are the gatekeepers who decide what is news.

TELEVISION NEWS AND ELDERLY PEOPLE

Studies and rating surveys agree that television news has become the public's most important source of information (Bower, 1985; Coulson & Macdonald, 1992; Iyengar & Kinder, 1987). Roper (1989) indicated 66% of those surveyed rely on television more than any other medium as their primary source of news. In addition, viewers feel the way television news is presented has improved over the years (Bower, 1985). Local television is rapidly becoming a prime source of news (Peale & Harmon, 1991). The people responsible for the news decisions that transform everyday events into the sights and sounds of the evening news-cast also are held responsible for building the public agenda of issues and events. If newspapers reflect society's concerns (Wass, Almerico, Campbell, & Tatum, 1984), then the same can be said for television news. Fisher (1977) said society's concerns do not include elderly people or the issue of aging.

Information about elderly people and issues of importance to them in televi-sion newscasts has been inadequate (Hess, 1974). Hess wrote that the media have missed "a truly big story" (1974, p. 84). The media have been charged with failing to capture the reality of being old in America, and with creating and rein-forcing negative stereotypes about old people (Bramlett-Soloman & Wilson, 1989; Gantz, Gartenberg, & Rainbow, 1980; Markson, Pratt, & Taylor, 1989;

Schramm, 1969). Although it is more than 30 years old, Wilbur Schramm's research (1969) still rings true: the media have overlooked the very fact of the emergence of elderly people as a major segment of the population.

Television news shows a tendency to be biased toward reporting events, especially catastrophes, rather than covering issues (Saltzman, 1979). Atchley (1991) wrote that network news, local news, and documentaries thrive on sensationalism. There is nothing sensational about people who successfully cope with everyday life. So, according to Atchley, those older people who are given attention in the news are those with "a problem that can be a springboard for human interest or commentary" (1991, p. 289). Aging and its inherent problems occur over time and usually are not associated with the simple situations which are characteristic of television news programming. The media also are accused of showing a bias against elderly people by failing to report information about aging (Powell & Williamson, 1985), leaving some elderly feeling socially insignificant and powerless.

In a study of television's effect on adults, Gans (1968) found that one third of the respondents felt that television helped them understand their personal problems and make decisions, particularly when they could identify with the situation being presented. Gans' findings suggested that examining television programming to identify messages about human life in general is appropriate, and can be applied to specific categories of individuals, such as older adults.

A number of studies have focused on gratifications sought and obtained from television news (Davis & Edwards, 1975; Rubin & Rubin, 1981; Wenner, 1984). These studies indicate that for some the content of newscasts provides information of value in personal and social situations. For others the process of viewing news may be an end in itself, because of its entertainment values and its ability to reduce feelings of social isolation. The television is readily accessible, provides a link to the outside world, allows the elderly to structure time periods of their day, and provides companionship.

Five gratifications have been identified (Palmgreen, Wenner, & Rayburn, 1980) which may provide insight into the television news viewing behaviors of the elderly. The five gratifications are as follows: a) general information seeking, b) decisional utility, c) entertainment, d) interpersonal unity, and e) para-social interaction. Local television news allows older people to seek highly useful community-based information. Disengaged from the mainstream of social life, many older people find the local news to be a source of amusement, human contact, and a substitute for "real-life" communication.

There are several reasons that local news may be the basis for social construction of reality perceptions by the elderly, beyond the fact that it is heavily watched and a part of regular daily activities. Local news is dramatic and often watched for entertainment reasons (Bogart, 1980; Dominick et al., 1975; Rubin, Perse, & Powell, 1985), and local news is perceived as realistic by much of its audience (Rubin et al., 1985). On an average evening a half-hour local newscast will have a slightly larger audience than a network newscast (Schonfeld,

1983; *Broadcasting*, March 30, 1987, pp. 163–164). Increased viewing of local television news does not mean an increase in the perception of personal safety (Perse, 1990), but it may influence an older viewer's thinking toward an issue of direct importance to him or her, for example, Social Security (Iyengar & Kinder, 1987).

Content analyses of network and local television newscasts show an absence of stories relating to social issues which might be of importance to elderly people (Stempel, 1988). Adams (1978) conducted an analysis of 10 Pennsylvania television stations, and found an emphasis on local politics, not on sensational and human interest stories. Nonpolitical community and organization activity received less than 1½ min of coverage, or about 9% of total news time. News framing represents selected reality (Tewksbury, Jones, Peski, Raymond, & Vig, 2000). Harmon found in a 1989 case study of Cincinnati that most of the stories fell into the police, fire, executive, and courts categories. Pollack (1989) argued that the media have done an incomplete job of educating themselves about social policy questions that affect the elderly. He said many editors see the problems of elderly people as too boring or depressing for regular coverage.

It may be that the problems facing elderly people are seen as boring or depressing because those problems are not viewed through the eyes of older Americans. In Gerbner's (1993) analysis of women and minorities on television, he found minority groups other than women were featured in only 3% of the network news stories analyzed. The news makers themselves were less likely to be older adults. Twelve percent of the male news makers were over 60 years of age, 6% of the women were over 60, and 1% or less of other minorities were over 60.

Of all the media, television offers the most frequent view of older people (Tebbel, 1975). Consequently, television is in a better position to eliminate misunderstandings. That has not been the case. In a Cable News Network special focusing attention on people 50 years of age and older (1993), gerontologist Ken Dychtwald noted that the media should be leading the charge in creating a more contemporary image of aging: "But the media, whether it's the movies or TV, are probably about 10 years behind." Sociologist Myrna Lewis (Cable News Network, 1993) said the media have an identity crisis: "They are faced with the demographics of their readership and their viewership, all of which are moving toward old age in enormous numbers. But, they cannot, personally, face this issue. So, I think they are denying the fact that the demographics are there and they cannot quite accept them, yet" (Cable News Network, 1993).

In a survey of television general managers and news directors (Hilt, 1997), several respondents focused on the content of television newscasts, and how it relates to the elderly. One respondent indicated that news content, not technological bells and whistles, will attract and keep an audience. Another respondent, a 36-year-old male general manager from a Top 30 market said, "Any complex issue is difficult to explain in a typical TV news format, not just issues facing older people" (Hilt, 1997, p. 69). A 39-year-old female news director said, "It's often difficult to get people on-camera to discuss issues of concern to the elderly—especially the elderly" (Hilt, 1997, p. 69). The Hilt (1997) study found that television general managers and news directors seemed to agree that older adults were an important part of the audience. However, the broadcasters have not changed their minds concerning the role of crime stories in their newscasts.

THE FEAR OF CRIME

The study of older people as crime victims has matured into one of the major areas of research in gerontology. Research on crime and the elderly centers on the victimization of older adults. Rosenfeld (1981) found that the elderly perceive more threat from crime and feel more threatened than younger people; change their activities in response to increases in crime more often than younger people; and, are far less likely to be victims of personal and property crimes, with the exception of larceny, than are younger people. Research by Levine (1986) found that major market local television newscasts include very substantial doses of helplessness. Members of the general public are most often presented as helpless, and by implication, so are most viewers. Helplessness is one common feeling experienced by victims of crime (Wallace, 1998).

OLDER CRIMINALS

As the older population increases in the United States, so has the number of older adults committing crimes. Because there are more elderly people, there are thus higher numbers of older adults apprehended and processed by the criminal justice system (Fattah & Sacco, 1989). Elderly offenders are being arrested more frequently than before as a result of growing intolerance toward their criminality. Shicor and Kobrin (1978) drew a link between the status of groups and the degree of criminal responsibility attributed to its members. Simply put, as the elderly grow in numbers and in status, they may incur a loss of any tolerance they may have enjoyed in the past (Fattah & Sacco, 1989).

CHAPTER SUMMARY

The field of gerontology provides a useful framework for understanding older adults use of and involvement with local television news. The routine activities of older people tend to be ignored by local television news, although older viewers are an increasing segment of the audience. Crime coverage, however, is important for newsrooms and salient for older viewers.

DISCUSSION QUESTIONS

1. What are the attitudes of television producers, assignment editors, and news directors toward elderly people? What are their perceptions about

issues of importance to elderly people? How might this influence the crime stories that are televised about elderly people?

2. How do elderly people's perceptions about crime differ from the statistics? How might this difference be explained?

3. How does the social disengagement theory explain local television news as important to older adults? Why is local TV news relevant to the elderly?

4. If you were a local television news director in your market, how would you cover elderly issues? What constraints exist that might limit attention paid to these concerns?

5. What impact do you think the aging of America will have on local television news broadcasts in the 21st century?

10

Television and the Future
of Local Crime News

*"Quality is decreasing because many 'new generation' television managers lack the eye
for detail and the seasoning that once gave stories extra depth and sensitivity."*

—Av Westin, Freedom Forum Fellow (Westin, 2000, pp. 4–5)

New technologies and new competition are dramatically impacting the local
television news environment. Most stations have adopted the recommendations of consultants to focus on news and information that attracts and maintains audiences. This often leads to an emphasis on live, on-scene reporting,
highly localized spot news, health and other features, as well as crime coverage.
The problem is that such coverage tends to be "episodic"and fails to place
events within a larger context (Gilliam et al., 1996).

Hard news crime coverage of dramatic and visual stories about violence in
the community are easy to tell within the extreme time constraints imposed by
local television news formats (Jamieson & Campbell, 2001). However, crime
stories often fail to explain the larger context of violent events. News coverage
of crime exaggerates violence because it makes up only one third of all crime:
"The overreliance on 'body bag' journalism distorts reality. Television news coverage of crime further distorts reality by exaggerating racial differences in the
propensity to commit different types of crime" (Gilliam et al., 1996, p. 19).

In contrast, a few news managers have charted a different course. They have
offered alternatives by breaking out of rigid news formats, leading with national
and international stories, providing longer and more contextual coverage, and
by emphasizing interaction with viewers.

LOCAL TV NEWS AND THE FUTURE OF CRIME COVERAGE

The Project for Excellence in Journalism in 1999 found that news directors see
a number of obstacles to improving quality of local television news: staffing,

139

Viewers Bill of Rights, by Forrest Carr

These days few would deny the relationship between journalists and the public is in trouble. Customers are trusting us less. They're watching less TV news and reading fewer newspapers. What do you do with any relationship worth saving when it falls into disrepair? You open a dialogue. You talk it out. You may even seek counseling.

In late 1998 and early 1999, KGUN9–TV in Tucson appointed a viewer ombudsman, launched a viewer feedback segment, and solicited public input for a statement of principles. With these steps we opened a dialogue with viewers. We're talking it out. We even have a counselor in the form of our ombudsman, Viewer Rep Heylie Eigen.

In response, viewers told us they were concerned about crime in their neighborhoods, but equally concerned about the relentless onslaught of negative news stories and the nightly parade of body bags. They told us they wanted privacy rights respected. They demanded to hear about solutions, not just problems. They asked us to conduct more investigations and ask tougher questions. By way of an employee committee, we weighed this input with our own notions of our journalistic duty, wrote the KGUN9 Viewers' Bill of Rights, and announced it on the air. Our contacts at the Poynter Institute believe we are the only television station ever to have solicited direct public input for a statement of principles, issued a document reflecting community values, and then provided a mechanism for public accountability.

Once a week Viewer Rep Heylie Eigen and I collaborate on a script dealing with viewer feedback. Anchors Colleen Bagnall or Guy Atchley share in the editorial process and deliver the copy on the air. Our viewers are not shy about hold-

Former KGUN news director Forrest Carr.

140

Heylie Eigen, KGUN viewer representative.

ing us to our promises. Occasionally they catch us doing something we shouldn't have. When this happens, we own up to it. Most importantly, they also shower us with story suggestions. We take many of them.

But wait a minute—this is not McDonald's. We're not here to take your order—are we? Heylie Eigen says, absolutely. "If they watch the news and still have questions, then obviously we're not doing our job." The difference is that now we have an opportunity to follow up and answer those questions. "They love it," says Heylie. And it's affected our product. "There are so many things we cover now that we never covered before."

This process is changing our newsroom culture. We're approaching our responsibilities differently. Here's an example: Recently the Tucson City Council voted to shut off half of this desert community's water wells because of pending EPA regulations on radon. Our competitors covered the story in the traditional "he says/she says" fashion, leaving viewers to sort out the conflicting statements and figure out the facts for themselves. But in our Viewers' Bill of Rights not only do we promise solution-oriented journalism, we say we'll ask the tough questions. So first we drew up a list of questions we wanted city officials to answer—and went so far as to read the list to our viewers. Then we proceeded to get those answers. At the same time, our reporters started digging. They found the threat from radon was not as severe as advertised and, in fact, the EPA was not asking for any well shutdowns. In the wake of our series of *Nine On Your Side* investigations, the city council reversed its decision.

Viewers responded enthusiastically. "It's definitely working," says anchor Colleen Bagnall. "They know we are the ones who do the investigating for them." Colleen adds this type of community-responsive journalism is important. "Sometimes we have this elitist attitude as journalists that we are only supposed to cover

KGUN news anchor Julie Myers during viewer segment.

traffic accidents and murder and 'be objective.' And while that is a part of our newscast, viewers want more out of it."

When we first announced this project some of our colleagues asked, "How will you respond when your viewers ask you to do something unethical or journalistically unsound?" We've discovered something interesting. We don't have to *agree* with our viewers. We just have to listen and, importantly, be willing to explain ourselves. "I engage them," agrees Colleen. "If you listen and give them your side, you win viewers over. I know you do. I've met people who say they've disagreed with something we did, but someone talked to them, they felt satisfied, and they continue to watch us."

In TV the ultimate question is this: Will it work in the ratings? The jury is still out, but there are some positive signs. Ratings have been mixed but have been trending upwards. We reached a major milestone in May 2000, when we tied longtime market dominator KVOA at 10 p.m. for the first time in memory. Moreover, our market research this summer revealed a turnaround in viewers' perception of KGUN9 so dramatic that our consultants initially thought they'd made a mistake.

Community-responsive journalism is not a magic bullet, of course. You must also win the big story, win weather, and have the right team of professionals in place to do it all. We believe we do. Heylie Eigen, who won a Lee Pacesetter award for customer service this year, is one of them. And she's loving every minute. "I have the greatest job," she says. "I really do. I love people." And if that's not what customer service is all about, what is?

Source: Forrest Carr, Correspondence with the Authors, June 18, 2000.

BOX 10.1   KGUN9's Contract with Viewers.

time, money, training, and the news hole. However, the standard responses given on the issue of quality do not acknowledge attempts to transform the nature of local news broadcasts.

WBBM, the CBS network-owned station in Chicago, beginning in February 2000, experimented with an alternative model of local television news. They were nicknamed by others as "PBS on CBS" because the station did stories as long as 20 minutes in length. The station challenged existing news formats by eliminating teasers for upcoming stories, floating weather and sports position with no set lengths, and returning to a solo anchor reporting hard news. According to anchor Carol Marin

> We haven't done a single story telling you who the real guy behind tonight's movie was. We haven't given you a disease of the week story based on some network programming. We haven't overblown weather. (National Public Radio, Morning Edition, April 4, 2000)

For example, on October 6, 2000, the station led with violence in the Middle East, as well as the Yugoslavian elections—a story they localized with a Chicago Serbian church service. The third story in the newscast briefly covered neighborhood tensions because of gang trouble. They used an over-the-shoulder

Carol Marin and WBBM, CBS 2 in failed TV news experiment.

YOU HAVE A RIGHT TO KNOW

KGUN 9 will ask the tough questions, conduct the investigations necessary and give the timely information needed to serve the public interest and protect public safety.

YOU HAVE A RIGHT TO ETHICAL NEWS GATHERING

KGUN 9 subscribes to the Society of Professional Journalists Code of Ethics, which requires journalists to seek the truth and report it, to minimize harm, to act independently and to be accountable.

YOU HAVE A RIGHT TO PRIVACY

Our journalistic duty and the public's right to know often require us to place people and organizations in the news who don't wish to be there. We will never do so in a cavalier or insensitive fashion and will always carefully consider privacy concerns as we weigh the importance of a story. We will never stalk or hound the victims of crime.

YOU HAVE A RIGHT TO POSITIVE NEWS

Much of the news our journalistic duty requires us to cover is by nature ugly. We will not filter out such stories in any way. However, we will take extra steps to find and report positive or uplifting stories which reflect the true character of life in our community. We will meet regularly with members of our community in order to discover those stories in person.

YOU HAVE A RIGHT TO RELEVANT CRIME COVERAGE

We recognize that an overemphasis on crime coverage would harm our community through portraying it in a false light of negativism. We will cover crime in such a way as to provide context, meaning, perspective and relevance. Before airing any crime story we will weigh its newsworthiness with the following questions:

- Is there an immediate danger or threat to the public?
- Is immediate action required?
- Is the safety or welfare of children involved?
- Is there a larger issue with public policy implications?
- Does the story touch, or should it touch, hearts in our community?
- Does the story spotlight a new crime trend or issue at the neighborhood level of which residents should be aware?

YOU HAVE A RIGHT TO SOLUTION-ORIENTED JOURNALISM

When appropriate we will be "On Your Side" and attempt to find or spotlight solutions to individual and community problems. We will help empower our viewers to better their lives and community.

YOU HAVE A RIGHT TO HOLD US ACCOUNTABLE

We will invite and respond to public input and feedback on our NEWS GATHERING decisions and philosophy. Our KGUN 9 Viewer Representative will serve as a viewers' champion within our newsroom. We will present and respond to viewer feedback within our newscasts on a regular basis. We will eagerly and diligently investigate complaints, publicly admit any mistakes and correct them prominently.

BOX 10.2   KGUN 9 Viewers' Bill of Rights.

graphic that asked the question, "gang WAR?" Carol Marin read the following: "Tonight, Chicago Police are disputing reports that two rival street gangs are in an all-out war in Lawndale." The station showed video of numerous police cars in force during a gang leader's funeral, a mug shot, an elementary school near where his murder took place, and a sound bite from a news conference with a deputy police superintendent. The station's fourth story that night was an in-depth investigation of a credit union, and then they went to a live shot in Seattle, WA, on the elimination of the Chicago White Sox baseball team from the playoffs. The station resisted the usual temptation to lead with gang violence or a local sports team story, although both were given significant coverage.

By fall 2000, the experiment was in trouble. The station's general manager and news director left, as did the assistant news director who helped design the program, after May ratings fell below two other local newscasts and reruns of "Friends" and "The Simpsons" on two independent stations (Johnson, 2000). John Callaway, a veteran TV journalist who left after doing commentary for the newscast, said he thought it was a shame that management did not support the program over several years. TV critic Ted Cox (2000) said the following: "The TV news is broken, and I admire anyone who is trying to fix it" (p. 10). He suggested that the newscast needed cosmetic changes to make it more eye-catching. However, on October 30, just 9 months after the experiment began, station executives pulled the plug. Marin sent a memo to colleagues saying, "I know that ratings are one measure of success. Fine work by excellent professionals is a truer measure. It's been an honor." The next day, the station returned to a more conventional 10 p.m. local news format. The return to a traditional local news format, however, produced even lower ratings. In the February 2001 sweeps, WBBM was down 22% at 10 p.m. from the year before. The station had a 5.2 rating and 8 share, compared with a 6.7 rating and 11 share in 2000.

The handful of news managers charting a new course for local television news said substance is more important than style. The goal appears to be to emphasize public affairs over breaking news, and to eliminate many of the ratings-driven and consultant-suggested features. As such, these new forms of local television news may move away from a heavy emphasis on crime coverage.

In the mid-1990s, KVUE–TV in Austin, TX, adopted five guidelines about crime coverage in which news managers asked five questions about any story to determine whether it should be aired:

- Is there an immediate threat to safety?
- Is there a threat to children?
- Does action need to be taken?
- Does the crime have significant community impact?
- Does the story lend itself to a crime-prevention effort? (*Nightline*, 1996)

KVUE has been Austin's top-rated television station for more than 4 years.

KGUN, Tucson, Arizona's, Channel 9 News Director Forrest Carr (2000) said his viewers do not like over aggressive "stick your camera into the tear-streaked faces" reporting from the scene of tragedies (p. 1).

The new and experimental models of local television news contrast sharply with the industry standard forged during the 1970s. Event-oriented and timely news coverage became the model for broadcast news as the industry developed. Viewers did not just learn about the story, they experienced it:

> Going live is exciting and dramatic. But is it good journalism? With live coverage now feasible from virtually anywhere at anytime, drama and excitement may overwhelm news judgment. Taste and common sense may be pushed aside in the rush to get on the air fast. The scrupulous allegiance to accuracy that should be the cornerstone of journalism is sometimes ignored because "there just isn't time" to check facts. (Seib, 2001, pp. ix–x)

Miami, FL, in the mid-1990s had a reputation of being the nation's leading example of crime-oriented local television news. NBC's Fred Francis, who once was a local reporter in Miami, said crime stories during the period crowded out stories about government:

> I grew up here. I learned my reporting on these streets. Crime reporting. Back then there was murder and mayhem. Lot's of it. But it didn't seem to crowd out all the other news as it does today. Today there are few beat reporters covering health, education and city politics. And there seems to be room for that kind of reporting because the murder rate is actually down. Way down from the city's deadliest year back in 1981. (Francis, *Dateline NBC*, January 26, 1994)

Francis said that public opinion polls at the time showed that South Floridians thought the murder rate was going up. He believed that the hype from local television news coverage was driving public fear.

In 1999, the Project for Excellence in Journalism studied Miami local television news along with 18 other markets:

> Miami is supposed to be the worst TV town in the country. WSVN is so notorious that its tapes are used in journalism schools as an example of the grotesque in local news. Things change. Miami's four major television stations have developed a culture of high enterprise, good sourcing, and a wide variety of stories.... WSVN is no longer "all crime all the time." The station airs the least crime at 6 p.m. Fusion now seems the approach—relentless coverage of breaking news, in-depth reporting, and consumer stories like "Help me Howard," a segment in which a local lawyer gives advice to viewers. (Parker & Leavitt, 1999, p. 91)

Over a 3-year period, the research group concluded that stations emphasizing "quality"—defined as less crime coverage, fewer gimmicks and more local issues—build ratings (Rosenstiel, Gottlieb, & Brady, 2000):

> ... A newscast should reflect its entire community, cover a broad range of topics, focus on the significant aspects of stories, be locally relevant, balance stories with multiple points of view, and use authoritative sources. (Rosenstiel et al., 2000, p. 87)

By contrast, profit-oriented stations that emphasize shortcuts tend to be judged poorly in terms of quality, and they tend to lose viewers over time. Unfortunately for local television news, a majority of stations appear to be hanging on to the tired model of emphasizing crime news and other breaking stories:

> Virtually all markets in the country place a premium on immediacy and the importance of live reporting from the scene. This usually means reporters stand in the dark, or at a crime scene, hours after the story has gone cold. (Dolan, 2000, p. 98)

The lack of creativity on the part of many newsrooms across the country, ironically, may be based on a false sense of security—a sense that the safest path is keeping the status quo model developed during the 1970s.

CHANGING REALITY THROUGH DIFFICULT CHOICES

The Alfred I. duPont Center and Newslab created a mock 30-min composite newscast that includes nine award-winning stories from six different local

TABLE 10.1

Local TV Web Site Ratings

Web Site	Station, Market	Adult Share
1. WRAL–TV.com	WRAL, Raleigh–Durham, NC	19.4%
2. Cincinow.com	WCPO, Cincinnati, OH	15.8%
3. 9News.com	KUSA, Denver, CO	12.8%
4. Newschannel5.com	WTVF, Nashville, TN	12.8%
5. Channel4000.com	WCCO, Minneapolis, MN	11.5%
6. WIStv.com	WIS, Columbia, SC	10.9%
7. 9Online.com	KWTV, Oklahoma City, OK	10.9%
8. KTVB.com	KTVB, Boise, ID	10.7%
9. KCCI.com	KCCI, Des Moines, IA	10.5%
10. KVUE.com	KVUE, Austin, TX	9.9%

Note. This is a list of top local television station Web sites. In early 2001, there were 345 TV Web sites identified in a survey, and more than half had attracted less than 4% of their markets. In Cincinnati, OH, Denver, CO, Des Moines, IA, and New Haven, CT, the top ranking TV Web site had more visitors than the local online newspaper. No studies have been done on the content of local television news Web sites.

Source: The Media Audit, http://www.lostremote.com, February 2001.

stations over a 2-year period. The model newscast does not include any traditional crime stories. According to Stuart Zanger, former news director at WCPO, Cleveland, OH, "It takes courage to lead with a 6 or 8 minutes story. It takes courage to lead with a story on school buses when ... everybody else is seeing stories about murders and deaths and fires and cars careening down the embankment" (Potter, 2000, p. 22). Among suggestions for local TV newsrooms are the following:

- *Break the mold*—Newsroom may be rewarded for taking creative risks.
- *Develop expertise*—Beat reporting may help reporters develop stories they would otherwise miss, and it also allows them to track stories over time.
- *Encourage enterprise*—Reporter-generated story ideas may produce more news on issues and trends.

- *Reward teamwork*—Team reporting may make time and space for quality journalism.
- *Support quality*—News manager needs to encourage quality journalism by de-emphasizing budget issues.
- *Take time*—Newsrooms should take more time in story development and presentation.
- *Understand the community*—Newsroom employees and managers who stay at their television stations longer tend to know their communities better, and can provide depth and context. (Potter, 2000, pp. 22–23)

The Project for Excellence in Journalism contended that "… a quality newscast would cover significant issues and a wide range of topics, would demonstrate local relevance and a high level of enterprise, and would include multiple, expert sources and various points of view" (Potter, 2000, p. 2).

THE INTERNET AND DIGITAL ACCESS TO CRIME NEWS

Local television news faces an important challenge from new media technology—cable news channels, Internet Web sites, and digital satellite feeds available in their markets. The dominance they once held is slipping, as evidenced by declining local TV news ratings in most markets. And, there is evidence that as local television stations ignore issues and localism, viewers will gravitate to the Internet (Rosenstiel et al., 2000). Thus, some local stations have created a Web presence and emphasized the new medium.

The emphasis on crime, dramatic video, and breaking news may or may not carry over to the online versions of their product. The television program Cybercrime is one example of the movement toward the use of local television news values on web sites. Recently, their online pages showed stories about jail cams (http://www.techtv.com). Although television programs continue to show interest in crime coverage, some Web sites such as crime.com have transferred completely the genre of news to the World Wide Web. One of the site's pages features "amazing video," "crime stories," and "dangerous chases" (http://www.crime.com). Crime coverage in cyberspace, however, may simply be a new way of communicating prejudice (Hecht, 1999; Power, 2000).

LOCAL TV NEWS

Critics of local television news would say that the reliance on crime and violent video is a turn-off for many viewers, but local TV news managers are quick to counter with the conventional wisdom that dramatic event coverage increases ratings. It is not clear whether alternative media will become a long-term challenger to local TV news, but it is true that most local TV stations are investing

TABLE 10.2

Local Market Interest in Streaming Media

Rank	City	Reach	Streaming Audience
1.	Miami, FL	43.1%	506,320
2.	Cincinnati, OH	41.0%	327,399
3.	Houston, TX	38.0%	670,745
4.	Pittsburgh, PA	37.9%	388,963
5.	Hartford, CT	37.7%	369,090
6.	New York, NY	37.4%	2,621,050
7.	San Diego, CA	37.4%	460,181
8.	Los Angeles, CA	36.9%	1,912,679
9.	Columbus, OH	36.9%	303,645
10.	Raleigh, NC	36.8%	266,376
11.	Portland, OR	36.7%	486,482
12.	Dallas, TX	36.7%	767,020
13.	Boston, MA	36.6%	1,084,770
14.	Seattle, WA	36.6%	738,582
15.	Cleveland, OH	36.5%	521,314
16.	Washington, DC	36.4%	897,155
17.	Orlando, FL	36.0%	441,942
18.	Chicago, IL	35.2%	1,068,256
19.	Indianapolis, IN	35.2%	349,839
20.	St. Louis, MO	34.9%	430,563

Note. The movement toward Internet-delivered video varies from city to city. In the next few years, local television news will be impacted by this trend.

Source: Nielsen//Netratings, March 2001; http://www.lostremote.com

in their own Web sites. Additionally, many local stations have formed cable news partnerships to have more outlets for their product. This allows them to participate in the technological revolution.

Crime has been a staple in the definition of news for more than a century. It will continue to be considered newsworthy. In the foreseeable future, it is likely that crime coverage will continue to be important for local television news. The presentation of crime news, including the use of dramatic and violent video, will no doubt be an ongoing controversy.

CHAPTER SUMMARY

In the final chapter of this book, the focus was on how some in the news business are looking for successful alternatives to the existing model of local television news. Specifically, efforts to offer viewers the opportunity to interact with newsroom employees is one way to change the status quo. The concern over the amount and type of crime coverage must be balanced against widespread public concern over crime as an important issue. At the same time, the public turns to local TV news as a key source for information. The appeal of crime news will not go away. Changes in the way local TV newsrooms do business must be substantive, and not just marketing ploys, to be meaningful. Event-oriented crime coverage should be placed within a larger context of what it might mean to the community. Spot crime news coverage tends to be dramatic, and it might heighten fears. However, such coverage does nothing to promote understanding about the causes of crime or the possible solutions. In-depth coverage that places a particular crime within a larger community context might help people engage in a discussion that leads to policy changes. In the end, the democratic model requires public participation in community life. The question for those interested in local television news is this—Can the change in the approach to covering crime satisfy both our social concerns and the industry bottom-line pressures?

DISCUSSION QUESTIONS

1. What are the obstacles to improving local television news?
2. What types of crime coverage guidelines have been adopted by newsrooms?
3. Do you believe that devices such as the Viewers Bill of Rights can have a positive impact on coverage? What are the limitations of such approaches?
4. What suggestions has the Project for Excellence in Journalism made to local newsrooms?
5. What suggestions would you make to improve local television news coverage of events in your community? Could the Internet be useful in making changes?

References

Adams, W. C. (1978). Local public affairs content of TV news. *Journalism Quarterly, 55*, 690–695.

Albarran, A. B. (1997). *Management of electronic media.* Belmont, CA: Wadsworth.

Allen, C. W., Lipschultz, J. H., & Hilt, M. L. (1998, August). *Local television journalism: Developing ethics through discussion.* Paper presented at the annual conference of the Association for Education in Journalism and Mass Communication, Radio–Television Journalism Division, Baltimore.

Altheide, D. L. (1985). *Media power.* Beverly Hills, CA: Sage.

Andersen, K. (1997). Gender and public opinion. In B. Norrander & C. Wilcox (Eds.), *Understanding public opinion* (pp. 19–36). Washington, DC: CQ Press.

Anderson v. Fisher Broadcasting, 12 Med.L.Rptr. 1604 (Ore. 1986).

Anderson, D. R., & Burns, J. (1991). Paying attention to television. In J. Bryant & D. Zillmann (Eds.), *Responding to the screen* (pp. 3–25). Hillsdale, NJ: Lawrence Erlbaum Associates, Inc.

Aronoff, C. (1974). Old age in prime time. *Journal of Communication, 24*(4), 86–87.

Associated Press. (2000, August 28). Violent crime down 10.4%, report says.

Atchley, R. C. (1991). *Social forces and aging.* Belmont, CA: Wadsworth.

Atkin, C. K. (1976). Mass media and the aging. In H. J. Oyer & E. J. Oyer (Eds.), *Aging and communication* (pp. 99–119). Baltimore: University Park Press.

Atkins, T. V., Jenkins, M. C., & Perkins, M. H. (1991). Portrayal of persons in television commercials age 50 and older. *Psychology: A Journal of Human Behavior, X*(x), 27–28, 30–37.

Babbie, E. (1998). *The practice of social science, (eighth edition).* Belmont, CA: Wadsworth.

Bae, H. S. (1999). Product differentiation in cable programming: The case in the cable national all-news networks. *The Journal of Media Economics, 12*(4), 265–277.

Bailey, F. Y., & Hale, D. C. (1998). *Popular culture, crime, and justice.* Belmont, CA: Wadsworth.

Baldwin, T. F., Barrett, M., & Bates, B. (1992). Uses and values for news on cable television. *Journal of Broadcasting & Electronic Media, 36*, 225–233.

Bantz, C. R., McCorkle, S., & Baade, R. C. (1980). The news factory. *Communication Research, 71*, 45–68.

Barak, G. (Ed.). (1994). *Media, process, and the social construction of crime.* New York: Garland.

Barrett, M. (1975). The Trojan horse: News consultants. In M. Barrett (Ed.), *Moments of truth? The fifth Alfred I. duPont–Columbia University survey of broadcast journalism* (pp. 89–112). New York: Crowell.

Barrow, G. M. (1996). *Aging, the individual, and society* (6th ed.). St. Paul, MN: West.

Barton, R. L. (1977). Soap operas provide meaningful communication for the elderly. *Feedback, 19*(1), 5–8.

Barton, R. L., & Schreiber, E. S. (1978). Media and aging: A critical review of an expanding field of communication research. *Central States Speech Journal, 29*, 173–186.

Baym, G. (2000). Constructing moral authority: We in the discourse of television news. *Western Journal of Communication, 64,* 92–111.

Bell, J. (1992). In search of a discourse on aging: The elderly on television. *The Gerontologist, 32,* 305–311.

Bennett, W. L. (1996). *The politics of illusion* (3rd ed.). White Plains, NY: Longman.

Berger, P. L., & Luckmann, T. (1966). *The social construction of reality.* Garden City, NY: Anchor.

Berkowitz, D. (1997). *Social meanings of news, a text-reader.* Thousand Oaks, CA: Sage.

Bishop, J. M., & Krause, D. R. (1984). Depictions of aging and old age on Saturday morning television. *The Gerontologist, 24,* 91–94.

Bitner, J. R. (1994). *Law and regulation of electronic media* (2nd ed.). Englewood Cliffs, NJ: Prentice Hall.

Blum, T. C., Roman, P. M., & Tootle, D. M. (1988). The emergence of an occupation. *Work and occupations, 15,* 96–114.

Blumstein, A. (1995). Prisons. In J. Q. Wilson & J. Petersilia (Eds.), *Crime* (pp. 387–419). San Francisco: ICS Press.

Boellstorff, L. (1996, June 27). Pace of executions quickens nationwide. *Omaha World-Herald,* p. 1.

Bogart, L. (1980). Television news as entertainment. In P. H. Tannenbaum (Ed.), *The entertainment functions of television* (pp. 209–249). Hillsdale, NJ: Lawrence Erlbaum Associates, Inc.

Bogdan, R. C., & Biklen, S. K. (1992). *Qualitative research for education.* Needham Heights, MA: Allyn & Bacon.

Bourdieu, P., & Coleman, J. S. (1991). *Social theory for a changing society.* Boulder, CO: Westview.

Bower, R. T. (1973). *Television and the public.* New York: Holt, Rinehart & Winston.

Bower, R. T. (1985). *The changing television audience in America.* New York: Columbia University Press.

Bramlett-Soloman, S., & Wilson, V. (1989). Images of the elderly in Life and Ebony, 1978–87. *Journalism Quarterly, 66,* 185–188.

Branzburg v. Hayes, 408 U.S. 665 (1972).

Broadcasting. (1987, March 30). TV makes more gains in latest Roper TIO Poll, 112(13), 163–164.

Broadcasting & Cable Yearbook 1999. New Providence, NJ: Bowker.

Brownstein, H. H. (2000). *The social reality of violence and violent crime.* Needham Heights, MA: Allyn & Bacon.

Burks, K. K., & Stone, V. A. (1993). Career-related characteristics of male and female news directors. *Journalism Quarterly 70,* 542–549.

Burton-Rose, D. (1998). *The celling of America.* Monroe, ME: Common Courage Press.

Cable News Network (1996, September 27). Racial tensions flare into fight at new Folsom Prison.

Cable News Network (1995, October 20). Alabama federal prison riot results in many injuries.

Cable News Network (1993, November 12). *Love, sex and romance after 50—Part 1.*

Campbell, C. P. (1995). *Race, myth and the news.* Thousand Oaks, CA; Sage.

Carelli, R. (1997, December 28). 1997 saw most executions since 1955. *The Associated Press.*

Carmichael, C. W. (1976). Communication and gerontology: Interfacing disciplines. *Journal of the Western Speech Communication Association, 40,* 121–129.

Carmichael, C. W., Botan, C. H., & Hawkins, R. (1988). *Human communication and the aging process.* Prospect Heights, IL: Waveland.

Carr, F. (2000). KGUN9's contract with viewers. Letter to authors.

Carroll, R. L., & Tuggle, C. A. (1997). The world outside: Local TV news treatment of imported news. *Journalism & Mass Communication Quarterly, 74,* 123–133.

Carroll, R. L., Tuggle, C. A., McCollum, J. F., Mitrook, M. A., Arlington, K. J., & Hoerner, Jr., J. M. (1997). Consonance in local television news program content: An examination of intermarket diversity. *Journal of Broadcasting & Electronic Media, 41,* 132–144.

Cassata, M. B. (1985). *Television looks at aging.* New York: Television Information Office.

Cassata, M. B., Anderson, P. A., & Skill, T. D. (1980). The older adult in daytime serial drama. *Journal of Communication, 30*(1), 48–49.

Cassata, M. B., Anderson, P. A., & Skill, T. D. (1983). Images of old age on daytime. In M. B. Cassata & T. D. Skill (Eds.), *Life on daytime television: Tuning-in American serial drama* (pp. 37–44). Norwood, NJ: Ablex.

Cassata, M. B., & Irwin, B. (1989). Going for the gold: Prime time's sexy seniors. *Media & Values, 45,* 12–14.

Caves, R. (1987). *American Industry: Structure, Conduct, Performance,* (6th ed.). Englewood Cliffs, NJ: Prentice Hall.

Chaffee, S. H., & Wilson, D. G. (1975, August). *Adult life cycle changes in mass media use.* Paper presented to the Association for Education in Journalism, Ottawa, Canada.

Chermak, S. M. (1995). *Victims in the news.* Boulder, CO: Westview.

Chermak, S. (1994). Crime in the news media: A refined understanding of how crimes become news. In G. Barak (Ed.), *Media, process, and the social construction of crime* (pp. 95–129). New York: Garland.

Christians, C., Fackler, M., Rotzoll, K., & McKee, K. (2001). *Media ethics: Cases and moral reasoning* (6th ed.). New York: Longman.

Chua-Eoan, H. (1998, May 11). Too many eyes in the sky? *Time,* p. 30.

Clary, M. (1997, March 26). Flames erupt in electric chair's death jolt. *Los Angeles Times,* p. A–1.

Clements, M. (1993, December 12). What we say about aging. *Parade,* pp. 4–5.

Cohen, A. A., Adoni, H., & Bantz, C. R. (1990). *Social conflict and television news.* Newbury Park, CA: Sage.

Collette, L., & Litman, B. R. (1997). The peculiar economics of new broadcast network entry: The case of United Paramount and Warner Bros. *Journal of Media & Economics, 10*(4), 3–22.

Comstock, G. A., Chaffee, S., Katzman, N., McCombs, M., & Roberts, D. (1978). *Television and human behavior.* New York: Columbia University Press.

Cook, J. (2000, May/June). Pulling the plug on the electric chair. *Mother Jones, 25,* 27.

Costanzo, M., & Costanzo, S. (1994). The death penalty: Public opinions, legal decisions, and juror perspectives. In M. Costanzo & S. Oskamp (Eds.), *Violence and the law* (pp. 246–272). Thousand Oaks, CA: Sage.

Coulson, D. C., & Macdonald, S. (1992). Television journalists' perceptions of group ownership and their stations' local news coverage. In S. Lacy, A. B. Sohn, & R. H. Giles (Eds.), *Readings in media management* (pp. 21–33). Columbia, SC: Association for Education in Journalism and Mass Communication.

Cox, T. (2000, October 12). With a few changes, Marin can still salvage her 10 p.m. newscast. *Daily Herald,* Sec. 4, p. 10.

Creech, K. C. (2000). *Electronic media law and regulation* (3rd ed.). Boston: Focal Press.

Creelman, J. (1896, May 17). World. In Folkerts, J., & Teeter, D. L., Jr. (1998). *Voices of a nation: A history of mass media in the United States* (3rd ed). Boston, MA: Allyn & Bacon, p. 269.

Creswell, J. W. (1994). *Research design: Qualitative and quantitative approaches.* Thousand Oaks, CA: Sage.

Crime Stoppers. (2001). Crime of the week, http://www.c-s-i.org/what.htm

Cumming, E., & Henry, W. E. (1961). *Growing old: The process of disengagement.* New York: Basic Books.

Dail, P. W. (1988). Prime-time television portrayals of older adults in the context of family life. *The Gerontologist, 28,* 700–706.

Daly, K., & Chasteen, A. L. (1996). *Feminism, media, and the law: Crime news, crime fear, and women's everyday lives.* New York: Oxford University Press.

Danowski, J. (1975, November). *Informational aging: Interpersonal and mass communication patterns at a retirement community.* Paper presented at the Gerontological Society, Louisville, KY.

Davis, R. H. (1971). Television and the older adult. *Journal of Broadcasting, 15,* 153–159.

Davis, R. H., & Davis, J. A. (1985). *TV's image of the elderly.* Lexington, MA: Heath.

Davis, R. H., & Edwards, A. E. (1975). *Television: A therapeutic tool for the aged.* Los Angeles: University of Southern California.

Davis, R. H., Edwards, A. E., Bartel, D. J., & Martin, D. (1976). Assessing television viewing behavior of older adults. *Journal of Broadcasting, 20,* 69–88.

Davis, R. H., & Kubey, R. W. (1982). Growing old on television and with television. In D. Pearl, L. Bouthilet, & J. Lazar (Eds.), *Television and behavior: Ten years of scientific progress and implications* for the eighties, volume II, technical reviews (pp. 201–208). Rockville, MD: National Institute of Mental Health.

Davis, R. H., & Westbrook, G. J. (1985). Television in the lives of the elderly: Attitudes and opinions. *Journal of Broadcasting & Electronic Media, 29,* 209–214.

DeFleur, M. L., & Ball-Rokeach, S. (1989). *Theories of mass communication* (5th ed.). New York: Longman.

DeFleur, M. L., & Dennis, E. E. (1996). *Understanding mass communication.* Boston: Houghton Mifflin.

del Carmen, A. (2000). *Corrections.* Madison, WI: Coursewise.

Delgado, F. P. (1998). When the silenced speak: The textualization and complications of Latina/o identity. *Western Journal of Communication, 62,* 420– .

Dennis, E. E., & LaMay, C. L. (1992). Crime story. *Media Studies Journal, 6,* xi–xvii.

Detweiler, J. S. (1987). Three newsgathering perspectives for covering an execution. *Journalism Quarterly, 64,* 454–462.

Dimmick, J. W., McCain, T. A., & Bolton, W. T. (1979). Media use and the life span. *American Behavioral Scientist, 23*(1), 7–31.

Dixon, T. L., & Linz, D. (2000). Overrepresentation and underrepresentation of African Americans and Latinos as lawbreakers on television news. *Journal of Communication, 50*(2), 131–154.

Dolan, T. (2000, November/December). News in prime time. *Columbia Journalism Review,* pp. 98–99.

Dominick, J. R., Sherman, B. L., & Messere, F. (2000). *Broadcasting, cable, the Internet, and beyond.* Boston: McGraw-Hill.

Dominick, J. R., Wurtzel, A., & Lometti, G. (1975). Television journalism vs. show business: A content analysis of eyewitness news. *Journalism Quarterly, 52,* 213–218.

Doolittle, J. C. (1979). News media use by older adults. *Journalism Quarterly, 56,* 311–317, 345.

Doppelt, J. C., & Manikas, P. M. (1990). Mass media and criminal justice decision making. In R. Surette (Ed.), *The media and criminal justice policy* (pp. 129–142). Springfield, IL: Thomas.

Downing, M. (1974). Heroine of the daytime serial. *Journal of Communication, 24*(2), 130–137.

Dychtwald, K., & Flower, J. (1989). *Age wave: The challenges and opportunities of an aging America.* Los Angeles: Jeremy P. Tarcher, Inc.

Eastman, S. T., & Ferguson, D. A. (1997). *Broadcast/cable programming, strategies and practices* (5th ed.). Belmont, CA: Wadsworth.

Ehrlich, M. C. (1995). The competitive ethos in television newswork. *Critical Studies in Mass Communication, 12,* 196–212.

Elliot, D. (1987). Creating the conditions for ethical journalism. *Mass Communication Review, 14,* 6–10.

Elliott, J. (1984). The daytime television drama portrayal of older adults. *The Gerontologist, 24,* 628–633.

Entman, R. M. (1994a). Representation and reality in the portrayal of blacks on network television news. *Journalism Quarterly, 71,* 509–520.

Entman, R. M. (1994b). African Americans according to TV news. *Media Studies Journal, 8,* 29–38.

Entman, R. M. (1992). Blacks in the news: Television, modern racism and cultural change. *Journalism Quarterly, 69,* 341–361.

Entman, R. M. (1989). *Democracy without citizens, media and the decay of American politics.* New York: Oxford University Press.

Epstein, E. J. (1973). *News from nowhere.* New York: Random House.

Estes v. State of Texas, 381 U.S. 532 (1965).

Fang, I. (1985). *Television news, radio news* (4th ed.). St. Paul, MN: Rada Press.

Fattah, E. A., & Sacco, V. F. (1989). *Crime and victimization of the elderly.* New York: Springer-Verlag.

Fisher, D. H. (1977). *Growing old in America.* New York: Oxford University Press.

Fishman, M. (1980). *Manufacturing the news.* Austin: University of Texas Press.

Folkerts, J., & Teeter Jr., D. L. (1998). *Voices of a nation, a history of mass media in the United States* (3rd ed.). New York: Macmillan.

Food Lion v. ABC, 116 F.3d 472 (1997).

Fox, K. A. (1997). An investigation of factors affecting job satisfaction and career motivation of on-air radio personalities. *Journal of Radio Studies, 4*, 30–44.

Francher, J. S. (1973). "It's the Pepsi generation ..." Accelerated aging and the television commercial. *International Journal of Aging and Human Development, 4*, 245–255.

Francis, F. (1994, January 26). *Dateline NBC.*

Freedburg, S. P. (1997, July 8). Is chair itself doomed? *The Florida Times-Union*, p. A–1.

Friedan, B. (1993). *The fountain of age.* New York: Simon & Schuster.

Gallup Poll. (2000). Crime tops list of Americans' local concerns [on-line]. Available: http://www.gallup.com.

Gandy, Jr., O. H. (1994). From bad to worse—the media's framing of race and risk. *Media Studies Journal, 8*, 39–48.

Gandy, Jr., O. H. (1982). *Beyond agenda setting: Information subsidies and public policy.* Norwood, NJ: Ablex.

Gandy, Jr., O. H., & Baron, J. (1998). Inequality: It's all in the way you look at it. *Communication Research, 25*, 505–527.

Gans, H. J. (1979). *Deciding what's news, a study of CBS Evening News, NBC Nightly News, Newsweek, and Time.* New York: Pantheon.

Gans, H. J. (1968). *The uses of television and their educational implications.* New York: The Center for Urban Education.

Gantz, W., Gartenberg, H. M., & Rainbow, C. K. (1980). Approaching invisibility: The portrayal of the elderly in magazine advertisements. *Journal of Communication, 30*(1), 56–60.

Geisler, J. (2000). *What it takes: Cultivating quality in local TV news.* Washington, DC: NewsLab.

Gerbner, G. (1993). *Women and minorities on television* (Research report). Philadelphia: University of Pennsylvania Press.

Gerbner, G. (1990). Epilogue: Advancing on the path of righteousness (maybe). In N. Signorielli & M. Morgan (Eds.), *Cultivation analysis* (pp. 249–262). Newbury Park, CA: Sage.

Gerbner, G. (1969). Toward "cultural indicators": The analysis of mass mediated public message systems. In G. Gerbner (Ed.), *The analysis of communication content* (pp. 123–132). New York: Wiley.

Gerbner, G., Gross, L., Signorielli, N., & Morgan, M. (1980). Aging with television: Images on television drama and conceptions of social reality. *Journal of Communication, 30*(1), 37–47.

Ghanem, S. (1997). Filling in the tapestry: The second level of agenda setting. In M. McCombs, D. L. Shaw, & D. Weaver (Eds.), *Communication and democracy* (pp. 3–14). Mahwah, NJ: Lawrence Erlbaum Associates, Inc.

Gilliam, Jr., F. D., Iyengar, S., Simon, A., & Wright, O. (1996). Crime in black and white, the violent, scary world of local news. *Press/Politics 1*, 6–23.

Gillmor, D. M., Barron, J. A., & Simon, T. F. (1998). *Mass communication law* (6th ed.). Belmont, CA: Wadsworth.

Gitlin, T. (1980). *The whole world is watching: Media in the making and unmaking of the new left.* Berkeley: University of California Press.

Glick, I. O., & Levy, S. J. (1962). *Living with television.* Chicago: Aldine.

Goedkoop, R. J. (1988). *Inside local television news.* Salem, WI: Sheffield Publishing.

Goodman, R. I. (1990). Television news viewing by older adults. *Journalism Quarterly, 67*, 137–141.

Graber, D. A. (Ed.). (2000). *Media power in politics* (4th ed.). Washington, DC: CQ Press.

Graber, D. A. (1997). *Mass media and American politics* (5th ed.). Washington, DC: CQ Press.

Graber, D. A. (1993). *Mass media and American politics* (4th ed.). Washington, DC: CQ Press.

Graber, D. A. (1980). *Crime news and the public.* New York: Praeger.

Graney, M. J. (1975). Communication uses and the social activity constant. *Communication Research, 2*, 347–366.

Graney, M. J., & Graney, E. E. (1974). Communication activity substitutions in aging. *Journal of Communication, 24*(4), 88–96.

Greenberg, B. S., Korzenny, F., & Atkin, C. K. (1979). The portrayal of the aging. *Research on Aging, 1*, 319–334.

Grey Advertising, Inc. (1988). The who and how-to of the nifty 50-plus market. *Grey matter alert.* New York: Grey Advertising.

Grossberg, L., Wartella, E., & Whitney, D. C. (1998). *Media making, mass media in a popular culture.* Thousand Oaks, CA: Sage.

Harmon, M. D. (1999). One consultant's effect on client TV news content. *Feedback, 40*(2), 22–28.

Harmon, M. D. (1989, August). *Featured persons in local television news.* Paper presented to the Association for Education in Journalism and Mass Communication, Washington, DC.

Head, S. W., Sterling, C. H., Schofield, L. B., Spann, T., & McGregor, M. A. (1998). *Broadcasting in America, a survey of electronic media* (8th ed.). Boston: Houghton Mifflin.

Head, S. W., Sterling, C. H., & Schofield, L. B. (1994). *Broadcasting in America, a survey of electronic media* (7th ed.). Boston: Houghton Mifflin.

Heider, D. (2000). *White news, why local news programs don't cover people of color.* Mahwah, NJ: Lawrence Erlbaum Associates, Inc.

Hermanson, L. W. (2000). The law in modern society. In W. W. Hopkins (Ed.), *Communication and the law* (pp. 1–19). Northport, AL: Vision Press.

Hess, B. B. (1974). Stereotypes of the aged. *Journal of Communication, 24*(4), 76–85.

Heyboer, K. (1999). Enhancing the integrity of electronic news. *American Journalism Review 21,* 14–15.

Hiebert, R. E., & Gibbons, S. J. (2000). *Exploring mass media for a changing world.* Mahwah, NJ: Lawrence Erlbaum Associates, Inc.

Hiemstra, R., Goodman, M., Middlemiss, M. A., Vosco, R., & Ziegler, N. (1983). How older persons are portrayed in television advertising: Implications for educators. *Educational Gerontology, 9,* 111–122.

Hilt, M. L. (1997). *Television news and the elderly.* New York: Garland.

Hilt, M. L. (1992). Television news and elderly persons. *Psychological Reports, 71,* 123–126.

Hilt, M. L. (1990, October). *Television coverage of the Starkweather homicides.* Paper presented at the Ike's America conference, Lawrence, KS.

Hilt, M. L., & Lipschultz, J. H. (1999). Revising the Kogan scale: A test of local television news producers' attitudes toward older adults. *Educational Gerontology, 25,* 143–153.

Hilt, M. L., & Lipschultz, J. H. (1996). Broadcast news and elderly people: Attitudes of local television managers. *Educational Gerontology, 22,* 669–682.

Holsti, O. R. (1969). Content analysis for the social sciences and humanities. Reading, MA: Addison-Wesley.

Horton, D., & Wohl, R. R. (1986). Mass communication and para-social interaction: Observation on intimacy at a distance. In G. Gumpert & R. Cathcart (Eds.), *Inter/media, interpersonal communication in a media world* (3rd ed., pp.185–206). New York: Oxford University Press.

Howard, E. (1996, July 17). Man executed in Nebraska's electric chair for killing boys. *The Associated Press* (Lexis–Nexis search).

Howitt, D. (1998). *Crime, the media and the law.* West Sussex, England: Wiley.

Husselbee, L. P. (1997). How reporters' role orientation may predict their ethical orientation. *Media Ethics 8*(2), 10, 22–24.

Illinois Press Association (2000). Blackouts. http://www.il-press.com.

Iyengar, S., & Kinder, D. R. (1987). *News that matters.* Chicago: University of Chicago Press.

Iyengar, S. (1997). Overview. In S. Iyengar & R. Reeves (Eds.), *Do the media govern?* (pp. 211–216). Thousand Oaks, CA: Sage.

Jackson, Sr., J. L. (2000). Race and racism in America. *National Forum 80*(2), 9–11.

Jacobs, J. (1990). *Changing channels.* Mountain View, CA: Mayfield.

Jacobs, J. (1977). *Stateville.* Chicago: University of Chicago Press.

Jamieson, K. H., & Campbell, K. K. (2001). *The interplay of influence* (5th ed.). Belmont, CA: Wadsworth.

Johnson, E. (1984). Credibility of black and white newscasters to a black audience. *Journal of Broadcasting, 28,* 365–368.

Johnson, S. (2000, September 22). Hold that hook! Yes, ratings are low, but Marin and Co. deserve time to click. *Chicago Tribune,* http://pgasb.pgarchiver.com/chicagotribune.

Jones, J. M. (2000, June 30). Slim majority of Americans think death penalty applied fairly in this country. [On-line] Available: http://gallup.com/poll/releases/pr000630.asp

Kaniss, P. (1991). *Making local news*. Chicago: University of Chicago Press.

Kappeler, V. E., Blumberg, M., & Potter, G. W. (1993). *The mythology of crime and criminal justice*. Prospect Heights, IL: Waveland.

Kent, K. E., & Rush, R. R. (1976). How communication behavior of older persons affects their public affairs knowledge. *Journalism Quarterly, 53*, 40–46.

Kerbel, M. R. (2000). *If it bleeds, it leads*. Boulder, CO: Westview.

Kidd-Hewitt, D. (1995). Crime and the media: A criminological perspective. In D. Kidd-Hewitt & R. Osborne (Eds.), *Crime and the media* (pp. 1–24). London: Pluto Press.

Klite, P., & Bardwell, R. A. (1997). Local TV news: Getting away with murder. *Harvard International Journal of Press/Politics, 2*, 102–113.

Koch, T. (1990). *The news as myth*. New York: Greenwood.

Kogan, R. (1992, August 14). Networks not following focus on older Americans. *Omaha World Herald*, p. 45.

Korzenny, F., & Neuendorf, K. (1980). Television viewing and self-concept of the elderly. *Journal of Communication, 30*(1), 71–80.

KTRK v. Turner, 987 S.W.2d 100 (1998).

Kubey, R. W. (1981). Television and aging: Past, present, and future. *The Gerontologist, 20*, 16–35.

Lacy, S., & Bernstein, J. M. (1992). The impact of competition and market size on the assembly cost of local television news. *Mass Comm Review, 19*, 41–48.

Lambeth, E. B. (1992). *Committed journalism* (2d ed.). Bloomington: Indiana University Press.

Lambeth, E. B., Christians, C., & Cole, K. (1994). Role of the media ethics course in the education of journalists. *Journalism Educator, 49*(3), 20–26.

Lang, A. (Ed.). (1994). *Measuring psychological responses to media messages*. Hillsdale, NJ: Lawrence Erlbaum Associates, Inc.

Lang, G. E., & Lang, K. (1984). *Politics and television re-viewed*. Beverly Hills, CA: Sage.

Lavrakas, P. J., Rosenbaum, D. P., & Lurigio, A. J. (1990). Media cooperation with police: The case of crime stoppers. In R. Surette (Ed.), *The media and criminal justice policy* (pp. 225–241). Springfield, IL: Thomas.

Levine, G. F. (1986). Learned helplessness in local TV news. *Journalism Quarterly, 63*, 12–18, 23.

Levinson, R. (1973). From Olive Oyl to Sweet Polly Purebred: Sex role stereotypes and televised cartoon. *Journal of Popular Culture, 9*, 561–572.

Levy, L. W. (1985). *Emergence of a free press*. New York: Oxford University Press.

Lieberman, S., & McCray, J. (1994). Coming of age in the newsroom. *Quill, 82*, 33–34.

Lind, R. A. (1993). Viewer response to ethical issues in television news. *Journalism Monographs, 142*.

Lippmann, W. (1922, 1965). *Public Opinion*. New York: Free Press.

Lipschultz, J. H., & Hilt, M. L. (1998). Local TV news and the death penalty: Social construction of a Nebraska execution. *Feedback, 39*(1), 21–30.

Lipschultz, J. H., & Hilt, M. L. (1993). First amendment vs. Business orientations of broadcast general managers and news directors. *Journalism Quarterly, 70*, 518–527.

Lipschultz, J. H. (1991). A comparison of trial lawyer and news reporter attitudes about courthouse communication. *Journalism Quarterly, 68*, 750–763.

Lipschultz, J. H. (1980). *Illinois prisons: Was Pontiac just the beginning?* Unpublished master's thesis, Sangamon State University, Springfield, IL.

Litman, B. R. (1980). Market share instability in local television news. *Journal of Broadcasting, 24*, 499–505.

Lotz, R. E. (1991). *Crime and the American press*. Westport, CT: Praeger.

Louis Harris and Associates, Inc. (1975). *The myth and reality of aging in America*. Washington, DC: National Council on Aging.

Louis Harris and Associates, Inc. (1981). *Aging in the eighties: America in transition*. Washington, DC: National Council on Aging.

Lowenthal, M. F., & Boler, D. (1965). Voluntary vs. involuntary social withdrawal. *Journal of Gerontology, 20*, 363–371.

Lull, J., & Hinerman, S. (1997). The search for scandal. In J. Lull & S. Hinerman (Eds.), *Media scandals, morality and desire in the popular culture marketplace* (pp. 1–33). New York: Columbia University Press.

MacNeil, R. (1996). *More news, lower standards*. Arlington, VA: The Freedom Forum.

MacNeil, R. (1968). *The people machine: The influence of television on American politics*. New York: Harper & Row.

Mares, M. L., & Cantor, J. (1992). Elderly viewers' responses to televised portrayals of old age. *Communication Research, 19,* 459–478.

Mark v. King Broadcasting Co., Wash. App., 618 P.2d 512 (1980).

Markson, E., Pratt, F., & Taylor, S. (1989). Teaching gerontology to the business community: Project older consumer. *Educational Gerontology, 15,* 285–295.

Martindale, C., & Dunlap, L. R. (1997). The African Americans. In B. A. D. Keever, C. Martindale, & M. A. Weston (Eds.), *U.S. news coverage of racial minorities* (pp. 63–146). Westport, CT: Greenwood.

McClellan, S. (1998). The ax men cometh. *Broadcasting, 128*(39), 6–7.

McLeod, J. M., Sitrovic, M., Voakes, P. S., Guo, Z., & Huang, K. (1998). A model of public support for First Amendment rights. *Communication Law and Policy, 3,* 479–514.

McManus, J. H. (1994). *Market-driven journalism*. Thousand Oaks, CA: Sage.

McQuail, D. (2000). *McQuail's mass communication theory* (4th ed.). London: Sage.

McQuail, D. (1994). *Mass communication theory, an introduction* (3rd ed.). London: Sage.

McQuail, D. (1985). Gratifications research and media theory: Many models or one? In K. E. Rosengren, L. A. Wenner, & P. Palmgreen (Eds.), *Media gratifications research* (pp. 149–167). Beverly Hills, CA: Sage.

Merrill, J. C. (1997). *Journalism ethics: Philosophical foundations for news media*. New York: St. Martin's Press.

Morgan, M., & Signorielli, N. (1990). Cultivation analysis: Conceptualization and methodology. In N. Signorielli & M. Morgan (Eds.), *Cultivation analysis* (pp. 13–34). Newbury Park, CA: Sage.

Moss, M. S., & Lawton, M. P. (1982). Time budgets of older people: A window on lifestyles. *Journal of Gerontology, 37,* 115–123.

Murphy, J. G. (1995). *Punishment and rehabilitation* (3rd ed.). Belmont, CA: Wadsworth.

National Public Radio, Morning Edition. (4 April, 2000). Late Night T.V.

Near v. Minnesota, 383 U.S. 697 (1931).

Nebraska Press Assn. v. Stuart, 427 U.S. 539 (1976).

Nelson, H. L., & Teeter, Jr., D. L. (1986). *Law of mass communications* (5th ed.). Mineola, NY: The Foundation Press.

New York Times v. Sullivan, 376 U.S. 254 (1964).

Newkirk, P. (2000). *Within the veil*. New York: New York University Press.

A. C. Nielsen. (1974, November). Nielsen estimates: National audience demographics report. *Nielsen '75*. Chicago: A. C. Nielsen.

Nightline (1996, September 24). Black and White: Race and local TV news (Transcript No. 4002–1). New York: ABC News.

Noelle-Neumann, E. (1995). Public opinion and rationality. In T. L. Glasser & C. T. Salmon (Eds.), *Public opinion and the communication of consent* (pp. 33–54). New York: Guilford.

Noelle-Neumann, E. (1986). *The spiral of silence, public opinion—Our social skin*. Chicago: University of Chicago Press.

Noelle-Neumann, E. (1984). *The spiral of silence, public opinion—Our social skin*. Chicago: University of Chicago Press.

Northcott, H. (1975). Too young, too old—Age in the world of television. *The Gerontologist, 15,* 184–186.

Nussbaum, J. F., Thompson, T., & Robinson, J. D. (1989). *Communication and aging*. New York: Harper & Row.

Ogles, R. M., & Sparks, G. G. (1989). Television violence and viewers' perceptions of criminal victimization. *Mass Communication Review 16,* 2–11.

Oliver, M. B. (1999). Caucasian viewers' memory of black and white criminal suspects in the news. *Journal of Communication, 49*(3), 46–60.

Orbe, M. P. (1998). An outsider within perspective to organizational communication: Explicating the communicative practices of co-cultural group members. *Management Communication Quarterly, 12*, 230–279.

Orbe, M. P. (1995). African American communication research: Toward a deeper understanding of interethnic communication. *Western Journal of Communication, 59*, 61–78.

Palmgreen, P., Wenner, L. A., & Rosengren, K. E. (1985). Uses and gratifications research: The past ten years. In K. E. Rosengren, L. A. Wenner & P. Palmgreen (Eds.), *Media gratifications research* (pp. 11–37). Beverly Hills, CA: Sage.

Palmgreen, P., Wenner, L. A., & Rayburn, J. D., II. (1980). Relations between gratifications sought and obtained: A study of television news. *Communication Research, 7*, 161–192.

Parker, D., & Leavitt, D. (1999). Miami vice no more. *Columbia Journalism Review, 38*, 91.

Passuth, P. M., & Bengtson, V. L. (1988). Sociological theories of aging: Current perspectives and future directions. In J. E. Birren & V. L. Bengtson (Eds.), *Emergent theories of aging* (pp. 333–355). New York: Springer.

Peale, B., & Harmon, M. (1991, August). *Television news consultants: Exploration of their effect on content.* Paper presented to the Association for Education in Journalism and Mass Communication, Boston.

Perkins, C. A. (1997). *Age patterns of victims of serious violent crime.* (Bureau of Justice Statistics Special Report.) Washington, DC: U.S. Department of Justice.

Perse, E. M. (1990). Cultivation and involvement with local television news. In N. Signorielli & M. Morgan (Eds.), *Cultivation analysis* (pp. 51–69). Newbury Park, CA: Sage.

Petersen, M. (1973). The visibility and image of old people on television. *Journalism Quarterly, 50*, 569–573.

Pettit, M. (1990). *A need to kill, final justice.* New York: Ivy Books.

Pew Research Center (1999). *Columbine shooting biggest news draw of 1999.* Washington, DC: The Pew Research Center For The People & The Press.

Pollack, R. F. (1989). Granny bashing: New myth recasts elders as villains. *Media & Values, 45*, 2–4.

Pollard, G. (1995). Job satisfaction among newsworkers: The influence of professionalism, perceptions of organizational structure, and social attributes. *Journalism & Mass Communication Quarterly, 72*, 682–697.

Pollard, G., & Johansen, P. (1998). Professionalism among Canadian radio announcers: The impact of organizational control and social attributes. *Journal of Broadcasting & Electronic Media, 42*, 356–370.

Power, R. (2000). *Tangled web: Tales of digital crime from the shadows of cyberspace.* Indianapolis, IN: Que.

Powers, A. (2001). Toward monopolistic competition in U.S. local television news. *The Journal of Media Economics, 14*(2), 77–86.

Powers, A., & Lacy, S. (1992). A model of job satisfaction in local television newsrooms. In S. Lacy, A. B. Sohn, & R. H. Giles (Eds.), *Readings in media management* (pp. 5–20). Columbia, SC: Association for Education in Journalism and Mass Communication.

Powers, M. H. (1992). *Saturday morning children's television and depictions of old age.* Unpublished master's thesis, University of Nebraska at Omaha.

Powell, F. C., Thorson, J. A., Kara, G., & Uhl, H. S. M. (1990). Stability of medical students' attitudes toward aging and death. *The Journal of Psychology, 124*, 339–342.

Powell, L. A., & Williamson, J. B. (1985). The mass media and the aged. *Social Policy, 21*, 38–49.

Press Enterprise v. Riverside County Superior Court, 478 U.S. 1 (1986).

Pritchard, D. (2000). Introduction: The process of media accountability. In D. Pritchard (Ed.), *Holding the media accountable* (pp. 1–10). Bloomington: Indiana University Press.

Quarderer, J. M., & Stone, V. A. (1989a). NDs and GMs define news 'profitability.' *Communicator, 43*, 10–12.

Quarderer, J. M., & Stone, V. A. (1989b). NDs and GMs describe their managerial 'marriages.' *Communicator, 43*, 32–34.

Radio–Television News Directors Association. (June 15, 2000). http://w2ww.rtnda.org/news/ 2000/abcfmminm.shtml

Radio–Television News Directors Association (2000). Keynote Speech, Christiane Amanpour. http://www.rtnda.org/news/2000/asera.shtml

Rahtz, D. R., Sirgy, M. J., & Meadow, H. L. (1989). The elderly audience: Correlates of television orientation. *Journal of Advertising, 18,* 9–20.

Ramsdell, M. (1973). The trauma of TV's troubled soap families. *Family Coordinator, 22,* 299–304.

Rawls, J. (1999). *A theory of justice* (Rev. ed.). Cambridge, MA: The Belknap Press.

Red Lion Broadcasting Co. v. FCC, 395 U.S. 367 (1969).

Reed, L. (2000, May 19). Anti-execution push parallels Nebraska's. *Omaha World-Herald,* p. 1.

Reese, S. D., & Buckalew, B. (1995). The militarism of local television: The routine framing of the Persian Gulf War. *Critical Studies in Mass Communication, 12,* 40–59.

Reinhardt, J. (2000). Baby boomers will be forced to stretch Medicaid dollars. *Messages, 7,* 1. Omaha, NE: Eastern Nebraska Office on Aging.

Reith, M. (1999). Viewing of crime drama and authoritarian aggression: An investigation of the relationship between crime viewing, fear, and aggression. *Journal of Broadcasting & Electronic Media, 43,* 211–221.

Richmond Newspapers v. Virginia, 448 U.S. 555 (1980).

Rogers, E. M., & Dearing, J. W. (1988). Agenda-setting research: Where has it been, where is it going? In D. A. Graber (Ed.), *Media power in politics* (4th ed., pp. 68–85). Washington, DC: CQ Press.

Roper Center (1999a, October 27). *News interest index poll.* Princeton Survey Research Associates, Storrs, CT.

Roper Center (1999b, June 15). *Americans' attitudes about the First Amendment survey.* Princeton Survey Research Associates, Storrs, CT.

Roper Center (1999c, February 12). *News interest index poll.* Princeton Survey Research Associates, Storrs, CT.

Roper Organization, Inc. (1989). *Public attitudes toward television and other media in a time of change* (Rep. No. 14). New York: Television Information Office.

Rosenfeld, F. H. (1981). Criminal victimization of the elderly. In D. Lester (Ed.), *The elderly victim of crime* (pp. 3–13). Springfield, IL: Thomas.

Rosenstiel, T., Gottlieb, C., & Brady, L. A. (2000). Time of peril for TV news. *Columbia Journalism Review, 6,* 84–89.

Roy, A., & Harwood, J. (1997). Underrepresented, positively portrayed: Older adults in television commercials. *Journal of Applied Communication Research, 25*(1), 39–56.

RTNDA (2000). *Covering hostage-taking crises, police raids, prison uprisings, terrorist actions* [On-line]. Available: http://www.rtnda.org/ethics/crisis.shtml

Rubin, A. M. (1982). Directions in television and aging research. *Journal of Broadcasting, 26,* 537–551.

Rubin, A. M. (1988). Mass media and aging. In C. W. Carmichael, C. H. Botan, & R. Hawkins (Eds.), *Human communication and the aging process* (pp. 155–165). Prospect Heights, IL: Waveland.

Rubin, A. M., & Rubin, R. B. (1981). Age, context and television use. *Journal of Broadcasting, 25,* 1–13.

Rubin, A. M., & Rubin, R. B. (1982a). Contextual age and television use. *Human Communication Research, 8,* 228–244.

Rubin, A. M., & Rubin, R. B. (1982b). Older persons' TV viewing patterns and motivations. *Communication Research, 9,* 287–313.

Rubin, A. M., Perse, E. M., & Powell, R. A. (1985). Loneliness, parasocial interaction, and local television news viewing. *Human Communication Research, 12,* 155–180.

Ryan, M., & Tankard, Jr., J. W. (1977). *Basic news reporting.* Palo Alto, CA: Mayfield.

Ryff, C. D., Marshall, V. W., & Clarke, P. J. (1999). Linking the self and society in social gerontology: crossing new territory via old questions. In C. D. Ryff & V. W. Marshall (Eds.), *The self and society in aging processes* (pp. 3–41). New York: Springer.

Saltzman, J. (1979). How to manage TV news. *Human Behavior, 8,* 65–73.

Scales, A. M. (1996). Examining what older adults read and watch on TV. *Educational Gerontology,*
22, 215–227.

Schonfeld, R. (1983). Pop news, TV's growth industry. *Channels, 3,* 34–38.

Schramm, W. (1969). Aging and mass communication. In M. W. Riley, J. W. Riley, & M. E. Johnson
(Eds.), *Aging and society, volume two: Aging and the professions* (pp. 352–375). New York: Russell
Sage Foundation.

Schreiber, E. S., & Boyd, D. A. (1980). How the elderly perceive television commercials. *Journal of*
Communication, 30(1), 61–70.

Seib, P. (2001). Going live, getting the news right in a real-time, online world. Lanham, MD:
Rowman & Littlefield.

Severin, W. J., & Tankard, Jr., J. W. (2001). *Communication theories: Origins, methods, and uses in the*
mass media (5th ed.). New York: Longman.

Shepard, A. C. (2000). Safety first. *American Journalism Review, 22,* 22–28.

Sherman, B. L. (1995). *Telecommunications management* (2nd ed.). New York: McGraw-Hill.

Shicor, D., & Kobrin, S. (1978). Criminal behavior among the elderly. *The Gerontologist, 18,* 213–218.

Shook, F. (1996). *Television field production and reporting, second edition.* White Plains, NY: Longman.

Signorielli, N., & Gerbner, G. (1978). The image of the elderly in prime-time television drama.
Generations, 3(1), 10–11.

Slattery, K. L., Hakanen, E. A., & Doremus, M. E. (1996). The expression of localism: Local TV news
coverage in the new video marketplace. *Journal of Broadcasting & Electronic Media, 40,* 403–413.

Smith, R. F. (1999). *Groping for ethics in journalism* (4th Ed.). Ames: Iowa State University Press.

Smolla, R. A. (1992). *Free speech in an open society.* New York: Knopf.

Sourcebook of criminal justice statistics 1998. Washington, DC: U.S. Department of Justice.

Splichal, S. (2000). Privacy and the professional communicator. In W. W. Hopkins (Ed.), *Commu-*
nication and the law (pp. 227–248). Northport, AL: Vision Press.

Stamm, K., & Underwood, D. (1993). The relationship of job satisfaction to newsroom policy
changes. *Journalism Quarterly, 70,* 528–541.

Steiner, G. A. (1963). *The people look at television.* New York: Knopf.

Stempel, G. H., III. (1988). Topic and story choice of five network newscasts. *Journalism Quarterly,*
65, 750–752.

Stempel, G. H., Hargrove, T., & Bernt, J. P. (2000). Relation of growth of use of the Internet to
changes in media use from 1995 to 1999. *Journalism & Mass Communication Quarterly, 77,* 71–79.

Stevens, L. A. (1978). *Death penalty, the case of life vs. death in the United States.* New York: Coward,
McCann & Geoghegan, Inc.

Stone, V. A. (2001). Majorities and women in television news. http://web.missouri.edu/~jourvs/
gtvminw.html

Stone, V. A. (1988). News directors move for professional advancement. *Communicator, 42,* 16–18.

Stone, V. A. (1986). *The changing profiles of broadcast news directors* (Unpublished report). Norman,
OK: Radio–Television Journalism Division, Association for Education in Journalism and Mass
Communication.

Sunstein, C. R. (1993). *Democracy and the problem of free speech.* New York: Free Press.

Super, D. (1980). The psychology of careers. In G. Esland & G. Salaman (Eds.), *The politics of work*
and occupations (pp. 112–117). Milton Keynes, UK: The Open University Press.

Surette, R. (1998). *Media, crime, and criminal justice* (2nd ed.). Belmont, CA: Wadsworth.

Surette, R. (1992). *Media, crime & criminal justice, images and realities.* Pacific Grove, CA:
Brooks/Cole.

Swayne, E., & Greco, A. (1987). The portrayal of older Americans in television commercials.
Journal of Advertising, 16, 47–54.

Tebbel, J. (1975). *Aging in America: Implications for the mass media.* Washington, DC: National
Council on Aging.

Tewksbury, D., Jones, J., Peske, M. W., Raymond, A., & Vig, W. (2000). The interaction of news and
advocate frames: Manipulating audience perceptions of a local public policy issue. *Journalism*
& Mass Communication Quarterly, 77(4), 804–829.

The Missouri School of Journalism (2000). *Guide to research on race and news.* Columbia: University of Missouri Press.

Thorson, J. A. (1995). *Aging in a changing society.* Belmont, CA: Wadsworth.

Trigoboff, D. (2000). Lessons of Columbine: Newspeople, recalling the horrors of Littleton, are learning to put saving lives first. *Broadcasting & Cable, 130,* 26–31.

Tuchman, G. (1978). *Making news, a study in the construction of reality.* New York: Free Press.

Tunstall, J. (1971). *Journalists at work.* London: Constable.

Tysver, R. (2000, May 8). Execution method rejected. *Omaha World-Herald,* p. 13.

Tysver, R. (1997, December 2). Man who killed 3 executed in Nebraska. *Associated Press Online* (Lexis–Nexis search).

Underwood, D. (1998). Market research and the audience for political news. In D. Graber, D. McQuail, & P. Norris (Eds.), *The politics of news, the news of politics* (pp. 171–192). Washington, DC: CQ Press.

Usdansky, M. L. (1992, November 10). "Nation of youth" growing long in the tooth. *USA Today,* p. 10A.

Vampola, K. A., & Hilt, M. L. (1996). A study of TV personnel's sources of occupational stress and interest in worksite stress management techniques. *Feedback, 37*(2), 7–11.

Vidmar, N., & Ellsworth, P. C. (1982). Research on attitudes toward capital punishment. In H. A. Bedau (Ed.), *The death penalty in America* (3rd ed., pp. 68–84). New York: Oxford University Press.

Wallace, H. (1998). *Victimology: Legal, psychological, and social perspectives.* Needham Heights, MA: Allyn & Bacon.

Wass, H., Almerico, G. M., Campbell, P. V., & Tatum, J. L. (1984). Presentation of the elderly in the Sunday news. *Educational Gerontology, 10,* 335–348.

Wenner, L. A. (1984). Gratifications sought and obtained in program dependency: A study of network evening news programs and 60 Minutes. *Communication Research, 11,* 537–562.

Wenner, L. A. (1976). Functional analysis of TV viewing for older adults. *Journal of Broadcasting, 20,* 77–88.

Westfeldt, W., & Wicker, T. (1998). *Indictment: The news media & the criminal justice system.* Nashville, TN: The First Amendment Center.

Westin, A. (2000). *Practices for television journalists.* Arlington, VA: The Freedom Forum.

White, W. S. (1991). *The death penalty in the nineties, an examination of the modern system of capital punishment.* Ann Arbor: University of Michigan Press.

Whitmore, R. V. (1995). *The portrayal of older adults in the New York Times and the Omaha World-Herald, 1982 and 1992.* Unpublished master's thesis, University of Nebraska at Omaha.

Wicks, R. H. (1989). Segmenting broadcast news audiences in the new media environment. *Journalism Quarterly, 66,* 383–390.

Wisely, W. (1998). California bans media interviews with prisoners. In D. Burton-Rose (Ed.), *The celling of America* (pp. 40–44). Monroe, ME: Common Courage Press.

Wolfe, D. (1987). The ageless market. *American Demographics, 9,* 27–29, 55–56.

Wu, W., Weaver, D., & Johnson, O. V. (1996). Professional roles of Russian and U.S. journalists: A comparative study. *Journalism & Mass Communication Quarterly, 73,* 534–548.

Wurtzel, A. (1992, March). *The changing landscape of network television.* Paper presented to the ABC television affiliate stations, New York.

Young, T. J. (1979). Use of the media by older adults. *American Behavioral Scientist, 23*(1), 119–136.

Author Index

Subject Index

A

ABC, 13, 27, 44, 49, 51, 54, 56, 58, 129,
     132–133
Advertising, 33, 132
Agenda Setting, 19–20, 132, 134
America's Most Wanted, 18, 84
Anderson v. Fisher Broadcasting (1986), 64
Assignment editors, 32, 36, 43–44, 134

B

Branzburg v. Hayes (1972), 61, 65
Broadcasting magazine, 136
Budget, 43, 134
     see *General managers*

C

CBS, 13, 15, 27, 44, 49, 51, 54, 56, 58,
     132, 143
     48 Hours, 103
CNBC, 130
CNN, 27, 49, 51, 54, 56, 58, 94, 96, 130,
     136
Columbine High Schools, 10, 51, 53,
     71–72, 83
Consultants, 15, 46
Crime Stoppers, 91, 93
Crime wave, 10
C-SPAN, 130
Culture and cultural studies, 1, 21–22, 102,
     113

Meaning making
     Cultivation, 20–21, 131

E

Elderly, 127–138
Electronic News Gathering (ENG), 13
Entertainment, 26, 135
Estes v. State of Texas (1965), 67–68
Event-centered, 22, 30
Eyewitnesses, 7, 22
     also see *Formats*

F

Federal Bureau of Investigation (FBI), 12,
     18
     Uniform Crime Reports (UCR)
First Amendment, 62, 93
Food Lion v. ABC (1997), 64
Foreign policy, 19
Formats, 5, 13
     Action news, eyewitness news
FOX News Channel (FNC), 27, 130
FOX Television, 18, 44, 132
Framing of news, 3, 19, 22, 25
Freedom Forum, 117
Furman v. Georgia (1972), 95

G

Gatekeeping, 29, 134
General managers, 34–36, 43, 134